D1536168

MAN-MADE
DISASTERS

Nuclear Accidents

Titles in the Man-Made Disasters series include:

Airplane Crashes

Nuclear Accidents

Oil and Chemical Spills

Shipwrecks

Tragedies of Space Exploration

MAN-MADE DISASTERS

Nuclear Accidents

Mark Mayell

LUCENT BOOKS®

THOMSON
GALE

San Diego • Detroit • New York • San Francisco • Cleveland • New Haven, Conn. • Waterville, Maine • London • Munich

LIBRARY OF CONGRESS CATALOGING-IN-PUBLICATION DATA

Mayell, Mark
   Nuclear Accidents / by Mark Mayell.
      p. cm. — (Man-made disasters)
Summary: Discusses the uses of radioactive substances and the dangers
they present, including fallout from nuclear weapons testing, the
meltdown at the Chernobyl power plant, and uranium mining accidents.
Includes bibliographical references and index.
   ISBN 1-59018-056-9
   1. Chernobyl Nuclear Accident, Chernobyl, Ukraine, 1986—Juvenile
literature. 2. Disasters—Environmental aspects—Juvenile literature.
3. Nuclear power plants—Ukraine—Chernobyl—Accidents—Juvenile
literature. [1. Chernobyl Nuclear Accident, Chernobyl, Ukraine, 1986.
2. Nuclear power plants—Accidents. 3. Radioactive substances.
4.Disasters.] I. Title. II. Series.
TK1362.U38M38 2004
   363.17'99—dc21

                                                                    2003010076

Printed in the United States of America

Contents

Foreword

In the late 1990s a University of Florida study came to a surprising conclusion. Researchers determined that the local residents they surveyed were more afraid of nuclear accidents, chemical spills, and other man-made disasters than they were of natural disasters such as hurricanes and floods. This finding seemed especially odd given that natural disasters are often much more devastating than man-made disasters, at least in terms of human lives. The collapse of the two World Trade Center towers on September 11, 2001, was among the worst human-caused disasters in recent memory, yet even its horrific death toll of roughly three thousand pales in comparison to, for example, the 1976 earthquake in China that killed an estimated seven hundred thousand people.

How then does one explain people's overarching fear of man-made disasters? One factor mentioned by the Florida researchers related to the widespread perception that natural hazards are "acts of God" that no one can control. Earthquakes, forest fires, and the like are thus accepted as inevitable. Man-made disasters are viewed differently, as unpredictable yet maddeningly preventable. Even worse, because these new technologies are so incredibly complex—a 747 airliner has 6 million parts, the 100-foot-long control room of a nuclear power plant has thousands of gauges and controls—the root cause of the disaster can often be shockingly trivial. One notorious 1972 airliner crash occurred when a tiny lightbulb, the indicator for whether the nose landing gear was down, burned out. While in flight, the captain, copilot, and engineer decided to replace the bulb. With the crew distracted, someone in the cockpit accidentally disengaged the autopilot and the plane flew into the ground, killing 98 of 176 onboard.

Man-made disasters are also distressing because they are so furtive in their deadliness. The hazardous radiation emitted by the nuclear accident at Tokaimura, Japan, in 1999 could not be seen or smelled, and the lethal gas that leaked from a Union Carbide pesticide factory in India in 1984 settled silently over the city of Bhopal, killing thousands in their homes.

Another factor may be the widespread perception that man-made disasters are much worse than ever. This is probably true although faulty designs and shoddy workmanship have been causing building collapses, dam failures, and ship sinkings for thousands of years. Beginning with the twentieth century, what is new is industrial technology, such as nuclear power and oil refining, that can affect huge areas over many years when something goes wrong. The radiation from the disaster at the Chernobyl nuclear power plant in 1986 spread worldwide and has closed local areas to human habitation to this day. Finally, man-made disasters have begun to compound each other: In January 1997, a massive oil spill caused by the shipwreck of a Russian tanker in the Sea of Japan threatened to clog crucial cooling systems in nearby nuclear power plants.

Fortunately, humanity can learn vital lessons from man-made disasters. Practical insights mean that ocean liners no longer ply the seas, as the *Titanic* did, with too few lifeboats and no ability to see in the dark. Nuclear power plants are not being built with the type of tin-can containment building that Chernobyl had. The latest generation of oil tankers has double hulls, which should vastly reduce oil spills. On the more philosophical level man-made disasters offer valuable insights into issues relating to progress and technology, risk and safety, and government and corporate responsibility.

The Man-Made Disasters series presents a clear and up-to-date overview of such dramatic events as airplane crashes, nuclear accidents, oil and chemical spills, tragedies of space exploration, shipwrecks, and building collapses. Each book in the series serves as both a wide-ranging introduction and a guide to further study. Fully documented primary and secondary source quotes enliven the narrative. Sidebars highlight important events, personalities, and technologies. Annotated bibliographies provide readers with ideas for further research. Finally, the many facts and unforgettable stories relate the hubris—pride bordering on arrogance—as well as the resiliency of daring pioneers, bold innovators, brave rescuers, and lucky survivors.

Disaster at Chernobyl

By far the worst nuclear accident in history started shortly after midnight on April 26, 1986, at the Chernobyl power plant in the Soviet republic of Ukraine. The facility had been built during the 1970s using a design that lacked some of the safety features in many other nuclear power plants. Most notably, Chernobyl's reactors were not enclosed in sturdy containment buildings, like the massive concrete domes seen at other nuclear plants. Such shells are able to trap any radiation that accidentally escapes from the reactor core, the site of the nuclear fuel.

The accident at Chernobyl was due to multiple operating mistakes that compounded the serious design flaws. The operators were shutting down one of the plant's four nuclear reactors, something that had to be done every year to perform routine maintenance. But plant managers decided this would be a good time to do an experiment, to see how much electricity could still be generated during the shutdown. This particular type of reactor, because of how its nuclear fuel was controlled, was more unstable at low power than high power. With crucial safety systems shut down, the technicians lost control of the reactor. The nuclear fuel started to melt and then exploded, dislodging a 2-million-pound roof slab and turning the reactor into a pile of rubble.

The explosion and subsequent fire caused a catastrophic release of radioactivity, high-energy rays and particles with potentially deadly effects. Thirty-one people died from the accident and rescue efforts, mainly firefighters who heroically sacrificed themselves to put out the raging nuclear fire. Thousands more people—the exact figure is hotly debated—

have died in the aftermath from increased cancer rates due to radiation exposure. Radiation blasted into the air above the destroyed reactor necessitated the evacuation of more than one hundred thousand nearby residents and left local towns and villages uninhabitable for decades. Toxic plumes that drifted toward Europe affected an estimated 4 million people.

Accidents on Land and at Sea

Could another Chernobyl happen? Many people think it is not only possible but also likely. Thirteen Chernobyl-type reactors remain in operation today, and nuclear technology is continuing to spread throughout the world. Thirty countries now operate 441 nuclear power plants, accounting for

◄ An aerial view of the ruined number four reactor at Chernobyl shows the extent of the damage from the April 26, 1986, explosion.

about 15 percent of the world's electricity. Moreover, some three hundred smaller research reactors are currently running in more than fifty countries. Such reactors serve a number of purposes, from being prototypes for nuclear power plant reactors to manufacturing radioactive products used for industrial and medical purposes, such as in cancer therapy machines.

Nuclear technology is also widely dispersed throughout the world's oceans, thanks to the more than 150 aircraft carriers, submarines, and other warships, as well as a few ice-breakers, that are powered by nuclear reactors. So far there have been a half-dozen accidental sinkings of nuclear-powered submarines. As "father of the nuclear navy" Admiral Hyman Rickover admitted, nuclear reactors on ships and subs are hardly foolproof. The "whole reactor game hangs on a much more slender thread than most people are aware," he once said. "All we have to have is one good accident in the United States and it might set the game back for a generation."[1]

▼ In a 1977 Department of Energy test of the safety of nuclear materials transport, a train traveling at more than eighty miles per hour strikes a spent nuclear fuel shipping cask on the bed of a truck.

Many of the military ships, of course, are carrying a second type of nuclear technology: nuclear bombs. The United States, Russia, and at least five other countries currently stockpile a total of about thirty thousand nuclear warheads worldwide, about two-thirds of which are considered operational. Although there have been no known accidental nuclear explosions to date, accidents involving nuclear weapons include lost bombs—at least fifty worldwide so far—and nuclear bombs that disintegrate (or have their conventional trigger explode, making them in effect a "dirty bomb") when planes carrying them crash. Then there are the accidental consequences, especially radioactive fallout, from the routine testing of nuclear weapons. Many of the individual tests the two superpowers, the United States and the Soviet Union, conducted during the 1950s released more radiation into the atmosphere than did the Chernobyl disaster.

An Ongoing Concern

Nuclear technology has spread well beyond the electric power and weapons industries. Various industries now use nuclear materials to trace chemical processes, diagnose and treat disease, and kill microorganisms on medical tools or food items. Consumer products that have radioactive components include smoke detectors and watch dials. Such commercial applications have occasionally resulted in contaminations, leaks, spills, and other nuclear accidents. "In addition to nuclear power plants," the Federal Emergency Management Agency admits, "hospitals, universities, research laboratories, industries, major highways, railroads or shipping yards could be the site of a radiological accident."[2]

Safety reforms instituted after Chernobyl may have decreased the risk of worst-case scenarios like core meltdowns, but nuclear accidents have been occurring since scientists began to discover the unique properties of radioactive substances more than a century ago. Within recent years concerns have grown about the possibility of lost, stolen, or abandoned nuclear materials falling into the hands of terrorists. As this complex technology becomes increasingly prevalent, humanity faces the urgent challenge of trying to prevent nuclear accidents.

CHAPTER ONE

Accidents Waiting to Happen

Nuclear technology by its very nature is highly complex, incorporating sophisticated mechanical as well as chemical technologies that make use of, and create as waste, substances that are highly toxic to all animal and plant life. Complex technologies require foresight and vigilance during their design, construction, and operation. They also demand constant and effective regulatory oversight, both by industry and government. Unfortunately, the history of nuclear technology suggests that such conditions frequently are not met. Moreover, even when they are met, accidents may still occur.

Inherent Dangers

Scientists in the early twentieth century were some of the first victims of nuclear accidents, since the immediate hazards—and the deadly long-term effects of radiation—were not initially well understood. Among the most famous victims was Marie Curie, the Nobel Prize–winning chemist who discovered the surprising, self-decaying properties of the element radium in 1898. Curie coined the term radioactivity, a property that had actually been discovered more or less by accident just two years earlier by the French scientist Henri Becquerel. He had noticed that an exposure appeared on a photographic plate that he had left on a piece of uranium-bearing crystal.

Along with her husband Pierre Curie, Marie devoted much of the rest of her life to studying radium, polonium (another radioactive element she discovered and named after her native country of Poland), and thorium. Pierre was showing signs of radiation sickness prior to his accidental death—he was run over by a horse-drawn carriage—in 1906. Marie also experienced health problems that, with hindsight, can be diagnosed as radiation-induced. She died at the age of sixty-seven of leukemia, a cancer of the blood cells that is now recognized as often being caused by radiation exposure. A number of medical journal articles written during the 1990s have tied Curie's death to her lifelong work with radioactive substances. She may also have been harmed by the radium pendant she sometimes wore, or by X rays, another type of radiation she experimented with during the 1920s.

Irène Joliot-Curie, the daughter of Marie and Pierre, also became a noted nuclear researcher before dying at age fifty-eight in 1956. Like her mother, Irène died from leukemia widely attributed to her radiation research. One estimate is that two out of every five early-twentieth century researchers in the new field of nuclear technology also died from cancers or suffered from radiation-related health problems.

The Many Faces of Radiation

Clearly these newly identified substances and technologies were unlike anything humanity had ever seen. Over the course of the past century researchers have investigated the

▼ Irène Joliot-Curie, one of a number of scientists whose death may have been related to nuclear research, operates the controls of France's first nuclear reactor at Fort de Chatillon, in the Paris suburbs, in 1948.

PARTICLES AND RAYS

Ionizing radiation comes in two basic forms, particles and rays.

Alpha particles are made up of two protons and two neutrons, elementary particles found in the nucleus of atoms. Alpha particles are relatively slow moving and do not have enough energy to penetrate, for example, paper or skin—although they may nevertheless harm the skin. They are most worrisome when a substance that emits them is eaten or inhaled, since alpha particles can then damage cells within the body.

Beta particles are single electrons, the elementary particles normally surrounding an atomic nucleus. Beta particles move at the speed of light and can penetrate paper and slightly into the skin. They cannot pass through, however, even a light metal such as aluminum.

Gamma rays are short bursts of high energy given off by an unstable atomic nucleus. They easily pass right through the human body and can even penetrate deep into lead and concrete.

unique radiation-emitting properties of some sixty substances found in nature and another two hundred human-made substances. Radioactivity is a natural decay process that involves the release of energy in the form of particles and rays. Some forms of radiation are much more powerful—and potentially harmful—than others.

Radiation in the most general sense refers to various types of energy that are released from a source into the surrounding space. Thus light and heat are forms of radiation. The type of energy given off by radioactive substances is a particularly powerful form called ionizing radiation. It is capable of penetrating to the atomic level and wreaking havoc on living cells.

Alpha particles, beta particles, and gamma rays are common emissions from radioactive substances such as uranium, plutonium, and cesium. Two additional types of ionizing radiation, X rays and neutrons, are not usually associated with natural radioactive decay processes. X rays come primarily from cosmic (outer space) sources; they can also be produced mechanically by bombarding a metallic target in a vacuum tube with fast electrons. X rays that pass through matter and strike a photographic plate provide a picture of objects of differing density. This is how medical X rays give doctors a clear picture of a broken bone. X rays are not as penetrating as gamma rays. Neutrons are emitted from the nucleus of substances such as uranium during nuclear chain reactions, as when a nuclear bomb is detonated. Neutrons can make other substances become radioactive.

Humans are exposed to low levels of ionizing radiation every day. This background radiation is mainly naturally occurring radiation such as from cosmic rays and from radioactive elements in soil and water. A smaller contribution comes from human-made sources such as medical X rays. The average American is exposed to about three hundred millirems (a millirem is one-thousandth of a rem, a measure of radiation dosage) of background radiation per year.

Diverse Applications

Scientists have identified a wide range of potential applications that take advantage of the energetic and penetrating powers of radioactive substances. For example, many of today's smoke detectors contain a tiny piece of the radioactive element americium-241. The americium-241 steadily releases alpha particles within a chamber containing oxygen and nitrogen atoms. When smoke particles enter this chamber, they interact with the alpha particles and the oxygen and

▼ Alpha particles emitted by radioactive polonium form a flower-like pattern in the center of a cloud chamber, a device for studying the movement of atomic particles.

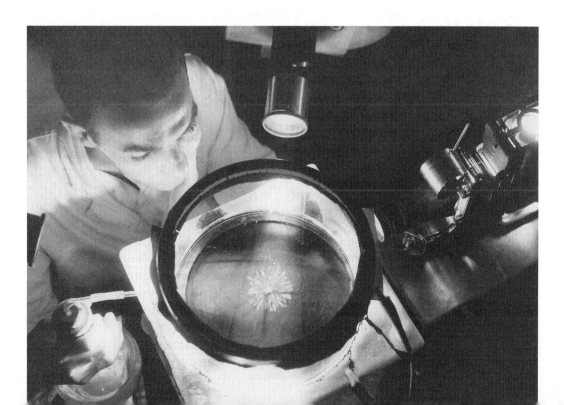

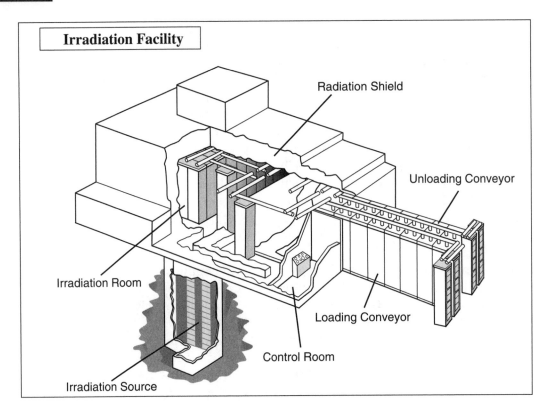

Irradiation Facility

Radiation Shield

Unloading Conveyor

Irradiation Room

Loading Conveyor

Control Room

Irradiation Source

nitrogen atoms in a predictable and measurable way that sets off the alarm.

Somewhat higher concentrations of nuclear materials are now being used for other applications. For example, irradiation facilities typically operate by placing medical devices, foods, or other products on a moving belt that passes through a "radiation room." When the product enters the radiation room, a radioactive source, such as cesium-137 or cobalt-60, is raised from beneath water and exposes the product to intense radiation. The radiation kills bacteria and other microorganisms, leaving the product sterile. Relatively high doses of radiation may be necessary. Meat, for example, may need to be exposed to three hundred thousand rads to kill most bacteria. (Rad, short for "radiation absorbed dose," is another common unit used to measure radiation.) This is well beyond the dose that would instantly kill any human, but not enough to make the meat itself radioactive. The source is then retracted and the belt moves the product out of the radiation room for shipment to industry or consumers.

Higher concentrations of radioactive materials have more potent properties that can be used to make nuclear weapons or to power nuclear reactors. This is because scientists have learned how to control fission and fusion, the splitting and combining of the nuclei in atoms. As the nuclei of elements such as uranium split or combine, they release tremendous amounts of energy.

Potent Effects on People

The particularly energetic radiation released by nuclear sub-stances can have various harmful effects on the body. Exactly what types of effects depends on numerous factors, includ-ing how much radiation the person is exposed to, the source of the radiation (which determines the type of particles or rays being emitted), and the duration of exposure. Two addi-tional related factors are whether the bodily exposure is ex-ternal or internal, as from ingesting or inhaling a radioactive substance, and what part of the body is affected. Radiation's

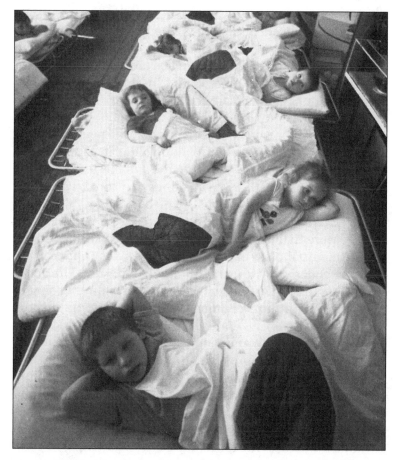

◀ Four years after the nuclear accident at Chernobyl, young chil-dren from a nearby collective farm await treatment in a hospital ward. Many suffer from intestinal problems tied to their radiation exposure.

IN THE AFTERMATH OF HIROSHIMA

The atomic bombings of Hiroshima and a second Japanese city, Nagasaki, in August 1945 have provided unique insights into the long-term health effects of nuclear radiation. *Hibakusha*, literally "explosion affected persons," is the Japanese term for atomic survivors. Over the last six decades, researchers have closely followed the lives of more than fifty thousand *hibakusha* with significant exposure to the bombs' effects. Studies have revealed that these *hibakusha* have about a 30 percent higher than normal chance of dying from cancer, including leukemia and cancers of the lungs, colon, stomach, and other organs. *Hibakusha* also suffer from higher rates of other diseases, although these have been more difficult to attribute directly to the effects of radiation. Persons exposed to bomb radiation before birth suffer from high rates of mental retardation. One hopeful, and surprising, finding has been that the children of *hibakusha* do not have higher than normal rates of damage to their chromosomes, the genetic building blocks.

most devastating effects are on the body's blood-forming organs, including the thymus, spleen, and bone marrow. The reproductive and the digestive organs are also very sensitive to radiation damage. Embryos and infants are more easily harmed by radiation than are adults.

The acute and long-term effects of radiation on a human population center were first seen when a U.S. plane dropped a fifteen-kiloton atomic bomb, equivalent to fifteen thousand tons of explosive TNT, on the Japanese city of Hiroshima on August 6, 1945. The massive shock wave and intense heat released by the blast killed some sixty thousand people (about 80 percent of whom were civilians) almost instantly. More than two hundred thousand city residents survived the initial blast but many of these were injured from building collapses, fires, and radiation exposure. The acute effects of radiation included internal organ failure, leading to worsening conditions characterized by symptoms such as weakness, nausea, and diarrhea. Radiation burns and damage to specific tissues and blood vessels necessitated amputations. Over the ensuing five months after the dropping of the bomb, as many as ninety thousand additional Hiroshima residents died from trauma and radiation effects. The total death toll since 1946, mainly from the long-term effects of radiation exposure, is more difficult to determine but is generally thought to be in the thousands.

The long-term effects of exposures to lower levels of radiation are more difficult to assess than the acute effects for any one individual. Again, multiple factors relating to radiation duration, intensity, and location determine whether health effects are felt immediately, twenty years later, or even not at all. Individuals can vary dramatically in how they respond to exposure, but scientists can more reliably predict the effects of certain exposure levels on a large population. These effects may include, for example, an increased risk of cancer and birth defects.

Since scientists first began considering the issue of safe levels of exposure to ionizing radiation more than fifty years ago, the trend has been toward lower and lower safety limits. For example, the internationally acceptable levels of annual whole-body exposure to radiation for workers were trimmed by 93 percent between 1934 and 1990. At least theoretically, many scientists now say that *any exposure* to ionizing radiation may possibly cause adverse health effects. Radiation may damage the nucleus of a single cell in the body, for example, in a way that allows the cell to reproduce in the damaged form and eventually, over many years, become a tumor. According to health physicist Karl Morgan:

> The question is not: What is a safe level? The question is: How great is the risk? All exposure subjects you to some risk. The more exposure you get to radiation, the greater the risk it will cause a cancer. The cancer may derive from one single small exposure, but on the other hand, it may derive from a series of exposures, one of which sometime in the past happened to be the actual cause.[3]

Tickling the Dragon's Tail

The unique nature of radioactivity means that it can lead to devastating accidents with potentially lethal effects. In fact deadly accidents began to occur as soon as scientists began to experiment with unleashing the atom's almost limitless energies. The first person to die from an acute exposure to radioactivity worked on the Manhattan Project, the U.S. government's Los Alamos, New Mexico–based effort to build the first atomic bomb during World War II. The nuclear chain reactions needed to create an atomic bomb's explosive force required especially concentrated sources of radioactivity. Scientists did not yet understand, however, exactly how potent

▲ Scientists unload plutonium hemispheres outside the George McDonald ranch house in 1945, in preparation for detonating the world's first atomic bomb at a New Mexico test site.

were these new human-made radioactive substances, such as the element plutonium.

In 1944 Harry Daghlian, a twenty-four-year-old graduate student in physics, went to work at Los Alamos with a more senior group of scientists. They became involved in a series of dangerous experiments involving a sphere of a form of plutonium known as plutonium-239. The idea was to gradually surround the sphere with tungsten carbide bricks that controlled the plutonium's ability to "go critical"—to become a self-sustaining nuclear reaction. The experiments were designed to come close to a critical reaction but not create one. Scientists referred to this as "tickling the dragon's tail."

Working late and alone on August 21, 1945, Daghlian accidentally dropped one of the tungsten carbide bricks directly onto the plutonium sphere. A blue glow immediately began to emanate from the plutonium as it released a sudden burst of energy and radiation. Daghlian quickly pulled the brick off the plutonium, noticing a tingling feeling in his hands. They had been exposed to a massive dose of radiation, on the order of ten thousand to forty thousand rems. His body had absorbed a fatal dose later estimated to be about five hundred rems.

Daghlian's month-long fight for survival, dramatized in the 1989 movie *Fat Man and Little Boy*, was medical researchers' first experience with acute radiation sickness. Within hours Daghlian's hands began to swell and become numb. Over the next few days in the hospital he experienced near-constant nausea and diarrhea, blistering and peeling of his skin, and abdominal pain after eating. Doctors realized that they could not treat Daghlian's condition. All they could do was to help alleviate some of his torturous pain. Daghlian died twenty-six days after the accident. The Los Alamos press office said that he died "from burns in an industrial accident,"[4] so it was some years before the true cause of his death became widely known.

Nuclear Follies

Despite almost six decades of nuclear experience since Daghlian's unfortunate death, and a much greater awareness of the risks involved, nuclear accidents continue to happen. The reasons typical of man-made disasters—poor facility design, equipment failure, lack of operator training, human error—usually combine to ultimately cause the accident. The most serious recent nuclear accident occurred at a Japanese nuclear fuel-processing plant. It was caused, like the Daghlian case, by the inadvertent combining of nuclear materials, allowing them to generate an ongoing nuclear reaction.

Like many of Japan's nuclear facilities, the JCO nuclear fuel production plant is located within an urban area, in this case the town of Tokaimura about ninety miles northeast of Tokyo. On the morning of September 30, 1999, two plant workers and a supervisor were supposed to put about five

ACCIDENTS WILL OCCUR

In the mid-1980s Yale University sociology professor Charles Perrow penned a highly influential book by the provocative title of *Normal Accidents*. In it Perrow argues that the dizzying complexity of much of modern technology, when matched with what he calls "tight coupling"—meaning processes happen fast and cannot easily be turned off—can inevitably lead to catastrophes. Nuclear power, Perrow notes, is especially vulnerable to such "system" or "normal" accidents. Moreover, piling on more and more safety features is not necessarily a solution because they add to the complexity, often in ways that are difficult to predict. Companies in such catastrophe-prone industries can train operators till they drop, Perrow says, but accidents will still happen.

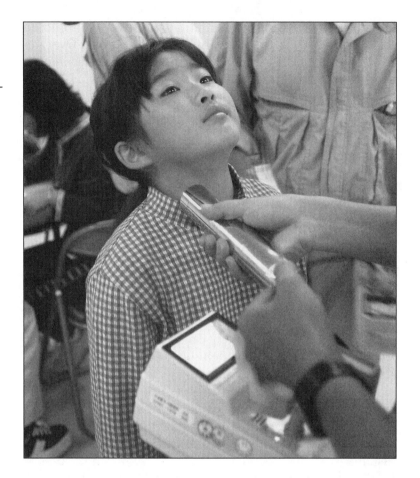

▶ A nine year-old child is checked for radiation levels after the October 1999 accident at the Tokaimura uranium processing plant in Japan.

pounds of a uranium compound into a series of storage tanks. Nitric acid in the tanks would purify the uranium so that it could be sold for use in nuclear fuel rods for a nearby reactor. The workers were not familiar with the task, which needed to be done only periodically, and had never handled this particular type of uranium. Events would show that their supervisor was similarly ill-prepared.

Bypassing a mechanized procedure, the workers loaded the uranium compound into buckets. They then dumped the uranium into a large precipitation tank rather than the smaller, narrower storage tanks mandated by procedural guidelines. They also put in about thirty-five pounds of uranium rather than the correct five pounds. All of these shortcuts were done with the supervisor's approval to speed up the whole process and thus cut costs. The improvised procedure quickly allowed the uranium in the precipitation tank to go critical. The two workers, next to the tank, saw a blue flash as neutron and gamma wave radiation surged out of the tank. The supervisor, in a nearby room, received a less massive dose of radiation.

A lack of effective emergency procedures allowed the reaction to continue for some twenty hours. It was not until almost three hours after the beginning of the accident that authorities began to evacuate people living and working within about a quarter-mile of the facility. Some three hundred thousand other people were advised to stay inside their homes. More than a dozen rescue workers who risked their lives to successfully stop the chain reaction, as well as several hundred paramedics, cleanup workers, and residents, were exposed to higher-than-normal levels of radiation. Radioactive contamination spread outside the plant before the reaction in the tank could be contained. In spite of round-the-clock care, the two workers died approximately three and six months later from acute radiation sickness.

Destined for Disaster

When the Japanese government's investigation was released less than three months later, many independent experts criticized it. The report called for increased worker education and training, an example of what has come to be known as the "blame the operator" syndrome. As technology scholar Charles Perrow has noted:

> Formal accident investigations usually start with an assumption that the operator must have failed, and if this attribution can be made, that is the end of serious inquiry. Finding that faulty designs were responsible would entail enormous shutdown and retrofitting costs; finding that management was responsible would threaten those in charge; but finding that operators were responsible preserves the system, with some soporific injunctions about better training.[5]

Tokaimura had developed what one source within the International Atomic Energy Agency (IAEA) referred to as "an appalling lack of safety culture."[6] Managers had not only let workers use the ill-fated illegal buckets, they shrugged their shoulders at the use of a portable electric cooking stove in the processing of the nuclear fuel. As a review by the Washington, D.C.–based Institute for Science and International Security noted, "The Tokaimura uranium refining plant did not have any markings identifying the site as dangerous, its staff lacked proper protective shields, it had no alarm system, and it had never been equipped with a safety manual."[7] At Tokaimura workers had routinely been told to cut corners to speed up the plant's production processes. The company had even written a secret procedures manual that it hid from government regulators, who themselves were shown to be rubber-stampers. The combination of complex technology and seat-of-the-pants operation seemed destined for disaster.

Losing Count

In the aftermath of the Tokaimura accident, an investigative task force of Japan's Nuclear Safety Commission said that Japan should drop the long-held myth that nuclear power operations are "absolutely safe." If such a myth is still widespread in Japan it has been increasingly recognized as a dangerous misperception in places that have more firsthand

▼ With Three Mile Island's cooling towers in the background, a U.S. Navy flatbed truck delivers lead bricks, useful for radiation shielding, in March 1979.

experience with nuclear accidents. The evidence suggests that such places are surprisingly widespread. The environmental group Greenpeace publishes a calendar listing all 365 days of the year as the anniversary of some accident or incident involving nuclear technology. For example, March 18: In 1987, fire and release of radioactivity at an Australian nuclear research facility. June 20: In 1985, collision of two trucks carrying nuclear bombs in Scotland. October 14: In 1953, fallout from British nuclear test "Totem" contaminates Aborigines in the Australian desert.

Determining exact numbers of accidents in the various categories, such as power plant accidents, weapons-related accidents, and irradiation facility accidents, can be difficult. Countries such as China continue to restrict reporting, for example. But estimates are possible. Meltdowns of a nuclear reactor are among the most serious accidents, as they can release a high percentage of their radioactive fuel into the environment. This cannot only endanger workers and nearby residents, it can potentially render a large area unfit for habitation for decades or even centuries. During a meltdown the reactor experiences a runaway chain reaction that results in overheating of the nuclear fuel and the melting of the core. The fuel can become so hot it is capable of melting right through the foot-thick steel floor of the reactor "pressure vessel," a kind of mini containment building that houses the reactor core with its nuclear fuel rods. This "China syndrome" scenario (so named because the melted core would presumably be dropping through the earth toward China) is accompanied by other dangers. As the U.S. Nuclear Regulatory Commission (NRC) notes, "Other possible dangers of a core meltdown were that the molten fuel would breach containment by reacting with water to cause a steam explosion or by releasing elements that could combine to cause a chemical explosion."[8]

There have been about ten such partial meltdowns in nuclear power plants and research reactors, ranging from the world's worst (Chernobyl) to lesser events in which small research reactors underwent partial meltdowns but did not release radiation into the environment.

Criticality accidents, like the recent one at Tokaimura, also can have grave consequences. Since 1945 there have been about two-dozen criticality accidents, including at least seven in the United States and twelve in Russia, with a score of fatalities. Nuclear accidents also include leaks and spills of radioactive materials that can injure people and contaminate the environment. These can happen during the processing, storage, and shipping of nuclear fuel as well as during the disposal of nuclear wastes.

Rating the Accidents

One of the first questions after an accident occurs is simply: How serious is this? As part of the international response to the Chernobyl accident in the late 1980s, a group of experts developed a seven-level "event scale" to classify the safety significance of incidents and accidents that happen at nuclear installations. The International Nuclear Event Scale (INES) has now become widely accepted by scientists in the field as well as by agencies including the NRC and the IAEA. The scale's main purpose is to put nuclear accidents into a perspective that allows the public to gauge their seriousness. Initially used just for accidents at nuclear power plants, the INES is now applied to accidents that occur in irradiation plants, at medical centers, and during transport of nuclear materials.

The scale ranges from 1 (least serious) to 7 (major accident). Dozens of level 1 and 2 events (equipment failures, for example, without likely health effects either to workers or to the general public) occur annually worldwide, mainly at nuclear power plants. The higher-rated accidents, causing injuries or deaths, garner worldwide publicity. For example, the accidents at Three Mile Island in the United States in 1979 and Windscale in the United Kingdom in 1957 were rated 5 (limited external release but major release of radioactivity within an installation). A 1957 explosion at a nuclear fuel reprocessing plant in the Soviet Union is the only level 6 event (serious accident with significant external release). Chernobyl is, so far, the only example of a level 7 event (external release of much of the radioactive material in a large facility, resulting in widespread health and environmental effects).

As can be seen, a number of the worst nuclear accidents in history have involved reactors. This is because reactors are complex to build and operate, and in order to run they need large quantities of concentrated radioactive materials. They also create highly toxic radioactive waste. The potential for disaster is thus ever-present.

CHAPTER TWO

From Meltdowns to Leaks

Hundreds of nuclear reactors have been constructed worldwide since 1942, when a University of Chicago team led by Italian-born physicist Enrico Fermi built the first reactor to achieve a self-sustaining energy release. Fermi was one of the pioneers of nuclear science and his reactor paved the way for the development of both the atomic bomb and the nuclear power industry. Because this was during World War II, the United States not surprisingly concentrated on building the atomic bomb. The world's first nuclear power plant did not begin to generate electricity for the Russian city of Obninsk until June 1954.

The nuclear power industry has taken off in the meantime. France depends upon nuclear power for about 75 percent of its electricity, and Japan, South Korea, Switzerland, and a few other countries for more than one-third. At least a dozen countries, particularly China, Japan, and South Korea, have plans to expand their nuclear power capabilities. As of mid-2003, some ninety new nuclear power plants are in either the planning or construction phase through 2016. Even in the United States, where no new reactors have been ordered since 1978, the year before the accident at Three Mile Island, the George W. Bush administration has said it is interested in reviving nuclear power as a major component of national energy policy. The 104 reactors in the United States nevertheless account for nearly one-third of the world's nuclear electricity.

A Concentrated and Dangerous Fuel

Reactor accidents are inherently dangerous in part because of the concentrated level of radioactivity in their cores and waste

▲ A painting captures the scene on December 2, 1942, at the University of Chicago when scientists observed the world's first nuclear reactor become self-sustaining. No photographers were present.

products. The nuclear fuel, typically uranium pellets packed into zirconium alloy rods, at a nuclear power plant holds huge amounts of radioactivity. For example, a large plant has perhaps 10 billion times the total radioactivity found in an average medical center's various cancer machines and radiological medicines. The energy release from a nuclear plant's fuel rods is typically moderated by using special control rods and a medium such as water.

Nuclear fuel rods remain exceedingly hazardous even after most of their usable fuel has been burned for generating electricity, since radioactive fission products remain bound inside the uranium pellets. Although these used fuel rods are referred to as "spent," in fact their level of radioactivity is up to a million times more concentrated than in a new fuel rod. Spent fuel rods are typically stored somewhere on-site for years, immersed in water to keep them cool and limit radiation release.

The shipping, use, and storage of this highly radioactive fuel and its waste products for power plant and research reactors have led to various types of accidents over the past half-century. These accidents have ranged from leaks that expose a single worker to low levels of radiation to meltdowns that have endangered surrounding communities. Even today, Perrow says, "Many processes are still not well understood, and the tolerances are frightfully small for some components."[9]

How best to contain and control the potent radioactive substances used in a reactor's core were sometimes learned only the hard way—by experience.

The 1957 Windscale Fire

Experimental reactors like Fermi's provided valuable insights but early nuclear facilities still had relatively primitive safety and engineering standards. This was certainly the case at the Windscale pile number one ("pile" was an early term for reactor). The British government had built Windscale on the site of an old ammunition factory on the Irish Sea in the late 1940s. Its purpose was to produce plutonium so that Great Britain could manufacture its own atomic bombs. The site's two reactor buildings were topped with what looked like square, 425-foot-high concrete chimneys. They functioned as chimneys, too, channeling the cooling air that had passed through the reactor core into the atmosphere. Windscale's design had two main drawbacks: It lacked a containment building and it made use of graphite—the soft form of carbon found in lead pencils—to control the reactor's core. To their dismay, scientists at Windscale ultimately discovered that graphite was capable of storing and releasing heat in difficult-to-predict ways.

On October 7, 1957, a Monday, Windscale operators started a process they had done more than a dozen times before to gradually release energy from the graphite in the core. Reactor number one was shut down. Numerous gauges and instruments were checked since these were needed to help operators carefully control the energy release. Even so, over the next three days the operators gradually lost control of the reactor. The rising temperature in the core could not be stopped. Finally, on Thursday, both the graphite and the uranium in the reactor's core caught on fire. Filters installed at the top of the massive chimney could no longer catch all the radioactive particles and gases being released. By Friday morning, after the fire had been burning for a full day, operators were becoming frantic. If the fire could not be brought under control, the facility and the surrounding area would have to be evacuated. As a last-ditch effort at quelling the fire, firefighters poured water down the chimney, praying that the whole facility would not blow up in a violent steam explosion. The water finally doused the fire, though the steam spilling out of the chimney added to the environmental contamination.

The huge cloud of radioactive steam released during the accident drifted as far as London, three hundred miles to the south. Dairy farms within an area of two hundred square miles of Windscale were shut down for two months, since radioactive iodine from the fallout was quickly identified as contaminating milk. Workers at the reactor, as well as some people who lived close to the facility, were exposed to radiation doses that were many times higher than then-current limits.

Gaps Revealed

The British government downplayed the true extent of the danger at Windscale and classified various documents as secret. Officials later admitted that vital safety information was kept from the public to prevent widespread fear and the loss of public confidence in nuclear power. They also admitted that "certain gaps in our scientific knowledge were revealed"[10] that needed to be addressed before Windscale-type reactors could be considered safe to operate.

In the mid-1980s an official British government report finally detailed the accident and attributed, over two decades, thirty-two deaths and at least 260 cases of cancer to the radiation releases. Other estimates of total deaths have ranged up to one thousand. Both of the Windscale piles were closed and sealed off after the 1957 accident; the damaged fuel in number one remained hot for decades. It was not until the late 1990s that remote-controlled robots could begin a multiyear project to safely dismantle the core for removal, treatment, and storage. The area is still the site of various nuclear facilities, though under a new name (Sellafield) with fewer connotations of disaster than Windscale.

HOW NUCLEAR PLANTS WORK

From the outside, power plants that use nuclear fuel look quite distinct from power plants fueled by coal or powerful rivers. These facilities actually function, however, in much the same way. Basically, they all heat water, converting it to steam. The resulting pressure turns the rotors in one or more turbines. The spinning turbine shaft powers a generator capable of producing electricity. Electrical current can then be sent, via high-voltage wires, to cities and towns.

Nuclear plants also feature elaborate cooling systems, since the nuclear fuel generates extensive heat that must be dissipated. Nuclear plants located on rivers or the sea use water as a coolant.

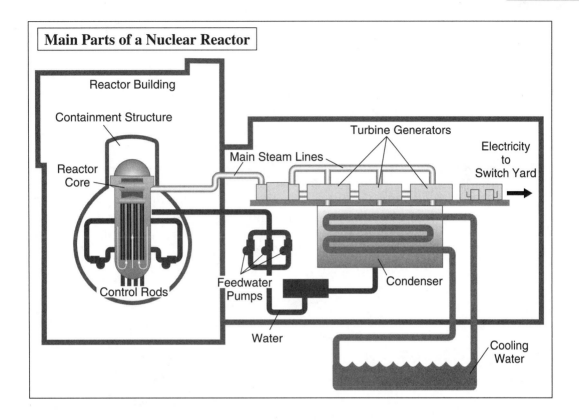

Main Parts of a Nuclear Reactor

Reactor Building

Containment Structure

Reactor Core

Control Rods

Main Steam Lines

Feedwater Pumps

Water

Turbine Generators

Electricity to Switch Yard

Condenser

Cooling Water

Perilous Research

Research reactors are much smaller than nuclear power plants and have less uranium or other fuel in the core. Thus, when accidents such as leaks and spills happen at research reactors, they do not approach the likes of Windscale in scope. On the other hand, research reactors typically experience more frequent start-ups and shutdowns compared to power reactors, increasing the chance for human error. Over the past fifty years there have been about a dozen serious accidents at research reactors, including at least three that resulted in fatalities.

The research reactor accident that caused the most deaths occurred on January 3, 1961, at the National Reactor Testing Station in Idaho Falls, Idaho. The station housed a small, experimental reactor run by the military. On the fateful day a three-man crew was inside the reactor vessel, on the top of the reactor. Their job was to manually withdraw control rods but only to a certain specified distance. For reasons that have never been determined, a control rod was taken out past the critical distance. Within a second the immediate power surge caused an explosion that released high levels of radiation into the reactor room. Two of the workers were killed instantly, including one man who was impaled by a control rod into the ceiling of the reactor room. (It was almost a week before his body could be removed, due to its remote position and the intense lingering radioactivity within the room that prevented sustained rescue efforts.) The third worker died within hours.

Many of the several hundred people called in for rescue and cleanup efforts also received high doses of radiation, including one worker who received an estimated 120 rems of whole-body exposure. Some radiation escaped into the environment before the reactor could be controlled. The three military technicians killed in the accident were so contami-

▼ Rescue crews needed to practice using this stretcher rig before attempting to retrieve the body of a worker impaled in the ceiling of an Idaho Falls reactor room in January 1961.

nated that the most irradiated parts of their bodies, such as their hands, had to be cut off and sent to a radioactive waste facility. What was left of the bodies still needed to be buried in lead-lined caskets inside metal vaults sunk ten feet into the ground. The ruined reactor building needed to be treated as radioactive waste as well.

Idaho Falls was a reminder that even relatively small nuclear reactors can be dangerous workplaces. The nuclear fuel in research reactors is moved somewhat more frequently than in power plants, another opportunity for accidents to happen. A 1983 fatality at a research reactor, at the Buenos Aires Critical Assembly facility in Argentina, was due to an accident during refueling.

A Candle in the Wind:
Blunder at Browns Ferry

Accidents at early power and research reactors had the beneficial effect of focusing engineers' attention on safety as reactors grew in size—and potential deadliness. A number of basic approaches to safety were identified relatively early on as crucial. Safety features needed to be redundant, with backup systems ready to kick in during emergencies. Plant designs incorporated "defense in depth" in the form of multiple protective barriers to prevent the release of radioactive materials. (The flimsy defense in depth, in the form of a weak containment building, was a major factor in why Chernobyl was a much worse disaster than the earlier one at Three Mile Island.) Systems also had a "single-failure criterion." For example, plans had to address the consequences of any individual pipe breaking or valve failing.

During the 1960s, when the first generation of large nuclear power plants was being built, these multiple approaches to safety were considered so foolproof that "worst conceivable disasters" (like meltdowns) were assumed to be impossible. This was a major factor that prompted, for example the U.S. Atomic Energy Commission (AEC), the forerunner to the NRC, to allow nuclear power plants to be located in major urban areas.

Thus, when the three-unit Browns Ferry nuclear power plant opened in Alabama in 1973, it was hailed as the largest—and supposedly safest—in the United States. Only two years later, however, on March 22, 1975, technicians at

Browns Ferry started a fire in a shaft carrying electrical wires. They had been using a candle to check for air drafts, an off-the-cuff procedure that violated various safety standards. The candle ignited the wires' insulation and was difficult to extinguish within the shaft. Local firefighters who were called in wanted to spray water on the wires but plant operators argued that this might compound the disaster. The fire disabled the controls that allowed operators to keep the reactor core cool with circulating water. Even worse, it also eventually disabled the emergency cooling system in unit one. Plant engineers scrambled to construct a makeshift cooling system that did narrowly manage to avert a core meltdown accident. "But the reactor was essentially out of control for several hours before firefighters prevailed," notes *Tritium on Ice* author Kenneth D. Bergeron, "finally extinguishing the blaze with the water hoses the plant manager had forbidden."[11]

The owners and operators of Browns Ferry, the federal Tennessee Valley Authority (TVA), had to shut down the plant for a year before repairs, mostly to unit one, allowed it to be restarted. The repairs cost taxpayers some $100 million. The TVA then operated Browns Ferry for a decade, experiencing various safety violations and accidents, including a leak of radioactive cooling water that contaminated the Tennessee River, before deciding in March 1985 to shut down all three problem-plagued reactors. Repairs and updates to units two and three allowed them to be restarted in 1991 and 1996, respectively.

Near-Disaster at Three Mile Island

Browns Ferry was, according to Bergeron, "the worst nuclear reactor accident in history, until it was eclipsed by TMI [Three Mile Island] four years later."[12] Like Browns Ferry, Three Mile Island was hailed as new and improved when the second of its two reactors was finished in the late 1970s. Although the number two reactor had experienced perhaps more than the usual start-up problems, on March 28, 1979, operators had it humming along at almost full capacity. They began to experience a baffling series of events, however, that ultimately was traceable to confusion about a single valve within the reactor's coolant system. This key "pilot operated relief valve" was supposed to be closed but was actually stuck open. Various automatic safety devices either did not work as planned, or were thwarted by operators who were unaware of the true state of affairs inside the reactor. Within two hours, the reactor's core was dangerously devoid of coolant. At the height of the emergency, more than sixteen hundred blinking lights and three audible alarms created a frantic scene in the control room. Before operators could figure out what was really happening, about half the core melted.

The accident at Three Mile Island came within perhaps thirty minutes of being a full-scale, China-syndrome-type meltdown. The containment building and the pressure vessel succeeded in keeping the radiation released by the melting core almost entirely within the facility. (There was a minor release to the environment and a temporary evacuation of local people.) Investigators ultimately determined that the accident was due to a combination of mechanical failure,

▼ Wearing protective boots, then President Jimmy Carter, center right, tours a Three Mile Island control room four days after the 1979 accident.

operator inexperience, deceptive control readings, and poorly designed equipment (at least one crucial gauge was not visible to operators). According to Bergeron:

> Nuclear reactors have some of the most reliable and redundant safety systems of any man-made facilities. But as TMI showed, systems can fail, people can err, and sometimes more than one thing can go wrong at a time. Despite clever design, careful manufacture, and dutiful maintenance, multiple failures of safety systems can and will occur.[13]

Author Charles Perrow agrees that what happened at Three Mile Island was not a freakish, one-in-a-million occurrence. He devotes an entire chapter in *Normal Accidents* to a close analysis of the accident and its "seemingly endless story of incompetence, dishonesty, and cover-ups before, during, and after the event." Yet, according to Perrow, "When we examine other accidents, the performance of all concerned—utility, manufacturer, regulatory agency, and industry—was about average. Rather sizable bits and pieces of the TMI disaster can be found elsewhere in the industry; they had just never been put together so dramatically before."[14]

The twelve-year cleanup of reactor number two at Three Mile Island cost $1 billion. Small amounts of nuclear fuel remain in the partially melted core but most of the reactor has been dismantled and shipped to waste sites. The number one reactor at TMI was restarted in 1985 and has operated without major incidents since then.

The Dreaded Scenario

The likelihood, if not inevitability, of an even more catastrophic nuclear accident was confirmed by the disaster at Chernobyl. One of the main reasons it had worldwide, rather than just regional, effects was due to design flaws in its reactors. Chernobyl was typical of five Soviet-designed nuclear power plants that went operational in Russia, Ukraine, and Lithuania during the 1970s and 1980s. The seventeen "RBMK" reactors at these plants were similar to plutonium-producing weapons reactors, and lacked a number of safety features common in conventional nuclear power reactors.

One flaw was that under certain circumstances, if coolant stopped circulating in the reactor vessel, the power in the nuclear fuel could feed upon itself. It could then increase to the point that the nuclear activity in the core became not the carefully controlled nucleus-splitting desired to generate electrical

WHAT BECOMES OF A MELTED CORE?

Few industrial accidents present as many repair and cleanup challenges as dealing with a melted reactor core. When a large power plant reactor melts, like at Chernobyl, immediate decontamination is not feasible—the building itself becomes a long-term waste site. Within a year at Chernobyl, engineers had used three hundred thousand tons of steel and concrete to enclose the entire ruined reactor in a twenty-four-story tomb. This sarcophagus had to be built using so-called "arms length" methods since workers were limited in how long they could stay near the highly contaminated site.

The radioactivity is so intense coming off the melted core of unit number four that even today this massive building does not stop it all. The hastily built structure is now showing signs of cracking, so Russian engineers have begun to build yet another containment building around it. Workers who go inside the tomb—widely regarded as the most radioactive building in the world—can stay for only two minutes before reaching their allowable exposure.

▲ Thirteen years after the 1986 accident, an official checks radiation levels outside the sarcophagus-enclosed Chernobyl reactor number four.

power, but the escalating chain reaction designed into nuclear bombs. Nuclear scientists say that most nuclear plants, including all those built in the United States, are designed to make this particular type of core meltdown impossible.

A second major flaw at Chernobyl was just as critical: The reactors lacked strong containment buildings. "What they had was a tin can,"[15] one critic commented. On the other hand, some experts say that the force of the 1986 explosion was so great that even the type of containment buildings common at the time might not have contained it.

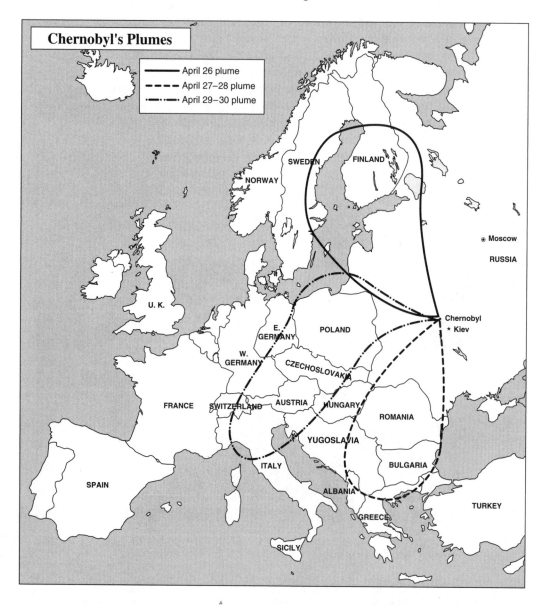

Chernobyl's Plumes

— April 26 plume
--- April 27–28 plume
·—·— April 29–30 plume

Warning: Do Not Enter

Scientists are still debating exactly how much radiation was released into the environment from the Chernobyl reactor's approximately two hundred tons of uranium fuel. Most current estimates range from about 100 to 200 million curies of radiation. (Named after Marie Curie, a curie is a unit of radioactivity equal to the radiation emitted by one gram of radium per second. This represents a potent level of radiation—the federal "maximum contaminant level" for radium in drinking water is 5 *trillionths* of a curie per liter.) Scientists are unsure because they do not know how much of the fuel in the core remains buried under tons of concrete, steel, and radioactive dust—perhaps only 80 percent or perhaps as much as 95 percent. The melted core remains much too radioactive to allow investigators in for a close look. Even the lower figure of 100 million curies represents one hundred times as much radiation as was released by the atomic bomb dropped on Hiroshima.

The radioactivity spewed from Chernobyl rendered a large area unsafe for human habitation. Two days after the explosion

▲ In December 2000, fourteen years after the accident, the Belarus town of Solnechny, near the Chernobyl nuclear power plant in Ukraine, remains deserted.

CHERNOBYL: THE FINAL TALLY

Researchers continue to argue about the total number of deaths that will ultimately be attributable to Chernobyl. The debate hinges on a number of unknown factors, including the total amount of radiation released and the likelihood of a given level of exposure ultimately causing a fatal cancer or other illness. One of the most widely quoted death tolls was twelve hundred, offered by Leonid Ilyin, vice president of the Soviet Academy of Medical Science, in 1990. This figure has since been challenged by new research that suggests the ultimate death toll is more likely to be upwards of fifteen thousand people. So far, there have been approximately two thousand cases of thyroid cancer among children who were up to fourteen years old in 1986, with perhaps five times as many cases expected in the future. This rate is much higher than normal. An estimated seventy thousand cleanup workers and Chernobyl-area residents suffer from radiation-related disabilities.

Soviet authorities organized an evacuation of the fifty thousand residents of Pripyat, the planned city built to accommodate the power plant. Within a week the fifty thousand residents of the eight hundred-year-old city of Chernobyl, nine miles distant, as well as another thirty-five thousand residents of seventy five small towns and villages inside a twenty-mile radius of the power plant, were also evacuated. As many as two hundred thousand additional people had to be temporarily evacuated, and in some cases relocated, from parts of Ukraine and Belarus, the Soviet republics that were exposed to the plume of radioactivity that spread in a northwesterly direction immediately after the accident. Some of these evacuated residents lived as far as three hundred miles from the site of the accident.

Seventeen years after the accident, Ukrainian officials still need to maintain an exclusion zone, officially known as the "Zone of Alienation," within twenty miles from the plant. Many of the residents of Pripyat and Chernobyl were moved into newly built towns such as Slavutich, located just outside the exclusion zone in an area that was less exposed to radiation. Plants and soils within the exclusion zone, as well as in other areas outside the zone, have higher-than-normal levels of radioactive substances such as cesium-137. The Zone of Alienation is not so radioactive, however, that people entering it face immediate and certain danger. Cleanup workers enter the area every day, and journalists and others visit. In recent years a few former residents have even moved back into their homes, although the Ukrainian government does not allow children to move in.

The other three reactors at Chernobyl, which were eventually restarted after the 1986 disaster, were shut down for good in 1991 (after a fire), 1997, and late 2000. Though much less contaminated than the destroyed number four reactor, they will also be highly radioactive even after the nuclear fuel is removed. Authorities expect to be doing cleanup work at Chernobyl for the entire twenty-first century.

The lost lives, the environmental damage, and the disrupted social networks are only part of the overall cost of the Chernobyl accident. The monetary drain is considerable. According to a 1990 study, "The 1986 accident at the Chernobyl nuclear plant cost the former Soviet Union more than three times the economical benefits accrued from the operation of every other Soviet nuclear power plant operated between 1954 and 1990."[16] During the 1990s the newly independent country of Ukraine had to devote 15 to 20 percent of its annual budget to Chernobyl-related costs.

New Pressures on Old Reactors

Safety reforms prompted by Three Mile Island and Chernobyl may have reduced the likelihood of disastrous, meltdown-type accidents. They have not made nuclear power plants foolproof, however. Within recent years a number of new risk factors have become evident. One is that many reactors built in the 1960s are now reaching the end of their expected lifetimes and thus may be more susceptible to mechanical failures. Another is that nuclear plants are facing increased pressure to cut costs in order to stay competitive with other forms of energy. Inappropriate cost-cutting may compromise public safety, as happened at the Millstone nuclear plant in Waterford, Connecticut, in the early 1990s. Operators tried to fix a damaged valve while keeping the plant functioning, saving millions in profits that would be lost during a shutdown. The plant had a brush with disaster when a bolt broke and radioactive steam billowed toward workers.

"We have not given the nuclear power generation system enough time to express itself," Perrow concludes, "and we are only just beginning to uncover the potential dangers that make any prediction of risk very uncertain."[17]

CHAPTER THREE

Weapons of Mass Destruction

The Cold War between American and Soviet interests that developed in the aftermath of World War II led to an arms race that was unprecedented in its potential firepower. Of the more than two thousand nuclear bombs exploded by seven nations since 1945, the United States and the Soviet Union set off almost half of these during the 1950s and 1960s. Nuclear bombs were being tested at a rate of every other day during 1962. By 1966 the U.S. stockpile of nuclear weapons reached a peak of approximately thirty-two thousand. Nuclear weapons installations run by the U.S. Defense and Energy Departments mushroomed in size and scope to the point where today they occupy more land than the state of Maryland.

Beginning in the early 1950s the U.S. government tried to put a more positive face on this fierce nuclear weapons race. The military conducted the "Ploughshares" test explosions to show that bombs could be used for peaceful purposes. (Scientists determined that bombs could potentially excavate canals, for example, but had a fatal drawback: They left behind a radioactive landscape.) "Nuclear bombs were depicted as palatable, even friendly," says *Nuclear Landscapes* author Peter Goin. "Small nuclear yields were called 'kittens.' The H-bomb, or hydrogen bomb, was also called the 'humanitarian bomb.'"[18] Popular magazines welcomed the nuclear age with predictions that Americans would soon be driving atomic-powered autos and heating their homes with atomic furnaces.

These public relations efforts were needed in part because there was much that was going wrong with the nuclear weapons industry. Although there has never been an accidental explosion of a nuclear bomb, there have been test-related hazards, extremely destructive accidents at government factories that convert uranium ore to bomb-grade plutonium, sunken nuclear submarines, and dozens of nuclear bombs that have been lost and never recovered. There have also been at least five instances in which nuclear weapons experienced an accidental explosion of their conventional (nonnuclear) trigger. The ultimate accident—terrorist use of a stolen bomb—remains in the realm of fiction even as the likelihood seems to grow.

Hidden Hazards of Atomic Testing

The 250,000 or so Japanese killed by atomic blasts in Hiroshima and Nagasaki were casualties of war. Those two episodes remain the only intentional use of nuclear weapons on people, though a few other individuals have died by accident during test explosions. Three such fatalities occurred on November 22, 1955, when the Soviet Union became the first country to explode a hydrogen bomb after dropping it from an airplane. "The bomb exploded underneath an inversion layer," notes an online history of the Soviet weapons program, "which focused the shock back toward the ground unexpectedly. This refracted shock wave did unanticipated collateral damage, killing three people from a building collapse."[19]

The United States has also experienced an accidental testing death. The Midas Myth 20-kiloton underground test conducted in 1984 caused the delayed collapse of a cavity, killing a technician who was measuring the effects of the blast.

▼ A late-1940s magazine illustration depicts a recovered paraplegic, "healed by atomic energy," smiling as he abandons his wheelchair and emerges from a mushroom cloud.

Raining Death from the Sky

Most of the potentially lethal hazards of atomic weapons tests are not from the blast itself but from the unintended after-effects of atmospheric explosions: the fallout of radioactive particles that the explosion launched into the atmosphere. (Perhaps as many as one in every three underground tests also releases radioactive gases into the air.) Although only about one-quarter of all nuclear weapons explosions have occurred in the atmosphere, the atmospheric tests involved much bigger bombs and thus account for about 80 percent of the total explosive power unleashed in nuclear tests. During the period of greatest atmospheric testing, from 1951 to 1962, an estimated 12 billion curies were released into the atmosphere. About three-quarters of all nuclear tests worldwide were conducted at either the Nevada Test Site (935 detonations) or at the Soviet's Semipalatinsk Test Site in Kazakhstan (496). As many as twenty-five Nevada tests released at least 150 million curies of radiation into the atmosphere, each one thus representing more radioactivity than many experts say was released during history's worst nuclear power plant accident, at Chernobyl in 1986.

The United Nations Scientific Committee on the Effects of Atomic Radiation has estimated that early aboveground nuclear weapons tests released about three tons of radioactive plutonium into the atmosphere. Because almost all of the atmospheric tests were conducted either in Nevada or in Kazakhstan, nearly 80 percent of this atmospheric plutonium was concentrated in the northern hemisphere. Populations that were downwind of the huge Nevada Test Site were especially at risk. The southwest Utah, mostly Mormon city of St. George even became known as "Fallout City" since, as photographer and author Robert del Tredici notes, "Testing policy determined that explosions take place when winds shifted away from highly populated areas like Las Vegas and toward sparsely populated areas like St. George."[20] The U.S. military exploded eighty-seven atmospheric nuclear weapons near St. George between 1951 and 1962.

Some of the 1950s atmospheric tests were so massive—one detonation was visible from eleven western states—that downwinders may have suffered almost immediate radiation-related ailments. For example, a 1997 report indicates that any farm children who drank goat's milk in a high fallout area were exposed to as much radiation, in the form of iodine-131,

as the worst-exposed children after the Chernobyl nuclear power plant accident. Author Cat Lazaroff notes that in the 1950s the U.S. government "informed photographic film producers of expected fallout patterns so they could protect their film supply, but did nothing to inform milk producers so that they could protect a vital component of the food supply."[21]

▲ In April 1952, the U.S. military allowed reporters and network cameramen to watch the explosion of a thirty-one-kiloton atomic bomb at close range.

The potential long-term adverse effects from multiple exposures to radioactive fallout are difficult to determine. Radiation-related illnesses, such as various cancers, take time to develop and could have any number of root causes. Yet medical studies have found that St. George has an overall rate of leukemia and other cancers that is much higher than that of other Mormons in Utah. The situation in the area around the Semipalatinsk site in Kazakhstan, where about one-third of almost five hundred nuclear explosions were aboveground, is even worse. Recently released records suggest that the Soviet military was aware of the deadly threat from radiation but used local villagers as nuclear war guinea pigs. "There's no place in the world that has inherited or suffered that kind of man-made disaster over a sustained period of time, affecting generations of people,"[22] says one UN official. According to *Toronto Star* reporter Allan Thompson:

> In 1997, nearly 500 of every 1,000 babies born in Semipalatinsk had some kind of defect or health problem and 47 of them died. In some regions, infant mortality has grown fivefold since 1950. In villages near the test site, up to 90 percent of people suffer from immune deficiency syndrome, leading to a virtual epidemic of tuberculosis.[23]

Estimates for the total number of deaths worldwide from cancers or lowered resistance to disease due to nuclear test fallout start at about fifteen thousand (from an analysis of government studies). A 1979 Nuclear Regulatory Commission report estimated that nuclear testing had killed between thirty-five thousand and eighty-five thousand people worldwide. Prior to 1963, when the United States and the Soviet Union agreed to a treaty that banned atmospheric tests, atmospheric blasts added about 7 percent to the dose of radiation naturally received as background radiation. No country has conducted an atmospheric test since China in 1980, and the 7 percent figure has now been reduced to about 1 percent.

A "Third Atomic Bombing of Japan"

The first person in the world to die directly from test fallout was probably Aikichi Kuboyama, a Japanese fisherman aboard the misnamed trawler *Lucky Dragon #5*. The fishing boat was exposed to fallout from the American military's Bravo test on February 28, 1954, conducted one hundred miles distant on the remote Bikini atoll in the South Pacific, midway between Hawaii and Australia. Kuboyama received

intensive medical treatment for liver and blood damage but died six months after exposure. Twenty-two other fishermen received exposures estimated at 300 rems, not much below the level (400 rems) that will kill about half of all people exposed. This "third atomic bombing" of Japanese people helped to start an antinuclear movement in the island nation.

Bravo, a fusion bomb, had been detonated on a reef in the atoll. Hydrogen bomb technology was still in its infancy and scientists were unsure of exactly how powerful Bravo would be. It turned out to be the most powerful bomb ever detonated by the United States, with a yield of about fifteen megatons—one thousand times more powerful than the atomic bombs that were dropped on Nagasaki and Hiroshima. Bravo vaporized three islands, left a crater a mile wide and two hundred feet deep, and threw radioactive debris over nearly fifty thousand square miles.

Some antinuclear activists claim that the Bravo test created the worst radiological disaster in U.S. history. The fallout from Bravo was so widespread that three hundred people

▲ In 1946 Bikini natives carry their possessions to U.S. Navy boats awaiting to evacuate them prior to nuclear testing.

RETURN TO BIKINI

Prior to 1946, the twenty-three islands of the Bikini atoll provided a home for a peaceable Marshall Islands community of 150 or so natives. When the U.S. government identified Bikini as an ideal nuclear testing site, however, the natives were moved. Over the next few years they became "nuclear nomads," since one island destination after another proved to have too little food or inedible fish.

The U.S. military set off some two dozen nuclear bombs on and around Bikini from 1946 to 1958. It was not until 1970 that U.S. authorities assured the people of Bikini that it was safe for them to return to the island. The natives' return proved to be short-lived. Within a few years tests showed that they had ingested dangerous levels of cesium-137 from the island's coconuts and other plant foods. Even though it is safe to live on Bikini if one eats only imported food, it was felt children would still eat the coconuts and ripe fruit, so in 1978 the atoll was once again cleared of its residents.

Within the past decade Bikini has come back to life as a scuba diving destination, with the main attraction being the many A-bomb-sunk warships. Tourists are warned that, almost half a century after the last nuclear test, the plant food remains unsafe to eat.

living on islands more than 150 miles away, as well as the twenty-three Japanese fishermen, were exposed to radiation that caused widespread sickness and one death. On Rongelap atoll, notes Bikini historian Jack Niedenthal, "Children played in the fallout and as night came they began to show the physical signs of radiation exposure. They experienced severe vomiting and diarrhea, their hair began to fall out, the island fell into a state of panic."[24] Authorities estimate that at least sixty islanders received doses of 175 rems. Test technicians and observers were also contaminated. U.S. authorities did not relocate Rongelap residents until three days after the blast, and the land remained unsuitable for human habitation until only recently.

The testing of nuclear weapons has declined dramatically since the early 1960s. Although more than four hundred nukes were set off underground during the 1980s, only fifty-eight tests were conducted during the 1990s. The United States has not set off a test explosion since 1992 and Russia since 1990. As of mid-2003, the last nuclear tests were conducted by India and Pakistan in May 1998.

Fearful Factories

The factories that concentrate uranium and construct nuclear weapons are another source of potential accidents. As the authors of "Cleaning Up the Nuclear Weapons Complex: Exploring New Approaches" have noted:

> The risks posed by the nuclear weapons sites are numerous, complex, and diverse. They derive from both hazardous and nuclear materials—and they result in risks to workers, the public, and the environment. There are known current risks, likely future risks, and risks associated with catastrophic events. In addition, there are sometimes risks to national security, as these facilities contain materials that could be used to make nuclear weapons.[25]

The U.S. nuclear facility that experienced many of the most publicized accidents was the Hanford Nuclear Reservation, in south central Washington State. The U.S. government relocated the three hundred citizens of the town of Hanford in 1943 to establish the vast complex. Among the site's main functions was to make the plutonium needed for the atomic bomb project. By 1955 the AEC had built eight nuclear reactors there as well as dormitories, storage tanks, and so forth. Although the site employed thousands of workers and encompasses more than five hundred square miles, the U.S. government was generally secretive about how much radiation its activities, both routine and accidental, released into the environment.

Washington-area residents began to understand the magnitude of the accidental contamination only after the Department of Energy took over Hanford in the 1980s and, responding to public pressure, began to release thousands of pages of previously classified documents. Scientists who analyzed the data determined that Hanford was probably one of the most radioactively contaminated sites in the nation. Hanford released about 750,000 curies of radiation into the air from 1944 to 1972, mostly in the form of iodine-131. Even higher levels, more than 20 million curies, were released into the waters of the Columbia River over the same time period. Most residents' exposure came from eating contaminated foods such as fish, drinking milk high in iodine-135, and breathing the radiation-polluted air.

Public concern about nuclear pollution, as well as the reduced demand for new nuclear weapons, took its toll on Hanford. By 1988 all of its reactors were shut down. Hanford was transformed from a production facility to a waste facility, an identity in which it had a head start. Today it stores about 60 percent of the nation's high-level radioactive waste.

Despite Hanford's new focus on cleanup, environmental recovery, and even historic preservation (there is talk of turning the B reactor, "an icon of the atomic age," into a tourist attraction), accidents on the site have continued into the new millennium. In May 1997 a chemical explosion blew the top off of a four-hundred-gallon tank in a room of the Plutonium Reclamation Facility, rupturing a water line and flooding the area with more than twenty thousand gallons of water. As the water surged through doors and out the building it carried radioactive material from contaminated areas of the facility into the environment.

Nature has also played a role in Hanford accidents: In July 2000 wildfires near Hanford spread to highly radioactive waste disposal trenches, raising airborne plutonium levels in the nearby cities of Pasco and Richland to one thousand times above normal.

Chelyabinsk's Checkered History

Hanford and a few other nuclear facilities, such as Colorado's Rocky Flats, are notorious in the United States but probably experienced fewer serious accidents than at similar facilities in the Soviet Union. The worst catastrophes occurred in secret cities that the Soviets built in the Chelyabinsk region in the southern Urals to manufacture nuclear weapons. From the mid-1940s until the demise of the Soviet Union in the late 1980s, Chelyabinsk was the site of three closely guarded government nuclear sites. Often referred to by

HANFORD'S "ATOMIC MAN"

One of the most famous single accidents at Hanford occurred on August 30, 1976, when worker Harold McCluskey was monitoring the extraction of americium-241 from some nuclear waste. Nitric acid reacted with the americium-241 and caused a chemical explosion that sprayed radioactive material in McCluskey's face. Colleagues who came to his rescue were also contaminated. The accident left McCluskey so radioactive he could set Geiger counters clicking from fifty feet away. During his treatment he had to live in a concrete-lined, windowless room in a special Hanford decontamination center. For a time all his urine and feces had to be collected and disposed of as radioactive waste. The local press dubbed him "the Atomic Man." He needed months of skin scrubbing to remove external radiation and took an experimental drug to remove internal contamination. Though the accident left him almost blind, McCluskey managed to live another decade before dying of heart disease at the age of seventy-five.

their postal codes (Chelyabinsk-40, -65, and -70), these secretive facilities were, like Hanford in the United States, major military-industrial complexes with tens of thousands of workers. Chelyabinsk-40, also known as Kyshtym for the nearby city, was the reactor complex where the Soviet military produced plutonium for its nuclear weapons.

▲ A pair of two-hundred-foot-tall reactor stacks falls in a simultaneous demolition carried out in August 1999 at the Hanford Nuclear Reservation in Washington.

Much like the American experience at Hanford, the Chelyabinsk nuclear sites dumped an alarming quantity of radiation into the environment for decades. The local Techa River, the main source of water for two dozen villages, became so radioactive from nuclear wastes that officials fenced it off—without admitting it posed a danger, of course.

In addition to such long-term contamination incidents, all three of the Chelyabinsk sites also experienced numerous accidents, with Chelyabinsk-40 leading the way. It has experienced at least three serious nuclear disasters, including a catastrophic explosion that was one of the worst nuclear accidents in history. It occurred on September 29, 1957, when a liquid waste storage tank malfunctioned. Pressure built up until it was released in a massive explosion. The radioactive cloud of pollutants that was blasted into the sky contained as many as 2 million curies of radiation. The toxic cloud drifted over more than two hundred towns and villages, contaminating the fields and water supplies of a quarter-million people.

According to a person who visited the "strange, uninhabited and unfarmed area" in 1961, "Highway signs along the way warned drivers not to stop for the next 20 to 30 kilometers because of radiation. The land was empty, there were no villages, no towns, no people, no cultivated land, only the chimneys of destroyed houses remained."[26]

Today about 80 percent of the contaminated land has been put back into use for farming and forestry. After the disaster, according to *Washington Post* reporter David Hoffman, "About 10,500 people along the Techa River were evacuated, but others were left behind. Efforts to track the health effects have been made years after the explosion, but the long delays have made it difficult. At all the sites, there has been little or no effort to clean up the radioactive contamination."[27] Many local people contend that the accident is responsible for elevated levels of cancer and birth defects in the area.

Yet another disaster occurred at Chelyabinsk-40 in 1967. In the 1950s Soviet officials started dumping highly radioactive liquid wastes into a shallow swamp instead of into the Techa River. This human-made waste lake eventually became known as Lake Karachai. Over the ensuing years the fifty-acre lake became increasingly radioactive. Russian officials recognized it as an environmental hazard and fenced it off from public access, but in 1967 a particularly hot summer nevertheless led to disaster. The lake dried up and high winds carried radioactive dust over a large area, forcing villages in the area to be evacuated. One estimate is that ten thousand square miles and five hundred thousand people were exposed to 5 million curies of radiation.

SHEDDING LIGHT ON THE MYSTERIOUS KYSHTYM EXPLOSION

Although tens of thousands of people in the Urals were aware of what had happened, news of the Kyshtym explosion was hushed up in the Soviet Union due to "national security." In the United States the Central Intelligence Agency learned about the incident but it kept as mum as the Soviets about it for two decades. The disaster was revealed to the world only in 1976 when Zhores Medvedev, an exiled Russian scientist, published a detailed account in the British journal *New Scientist*. Even then, many nuclear experts dismissed the report as a dissident's exaggeration. Within a matter of weeks, however, newspaper reports had confirmed Medvedev's account, which he later expanded in the book *Nuclear Disaster in the Urals*.

The Double-Whammy of Nuclear Submarine Disasters

When the Russian submarine *Kursk* sank on August 12, 2000, with the loss of 118 lives, it was the sixth nuclear-powered submarine to end up on the floor of the ocean. This includes two U.S. subs, *Thresher* and *Scorpion*, lost during the 1960s. The 129 sailors lost when the *Thresher* went to the bottom make it the worst submarine disaster in history, one that may have at least indirectly been due to an accident involving the ship's nuclear reactor. Nuclear subs that sink can represent a threat to the environment both from their reactors and from the nuclear weapons they may have onboard. Indeed the very proximity of these two technologies (not to mention the rocket fueled missiles themselves) found in a small space adds to the risk.

Nuclear subs also present dangers from their routine operation. One of the best known incidents—thanks to a 2002 feature movie—occurred in 1961 on the Soviet sub K-19. K-19's reactor was threatened with the loss of its cooling system when a pipe developed a leak while the sub was in the North Atlantic. The ship's engineers figured out a way to rig a temporary supply of coolant, thus preventing an uncontrolled chain reaction and a potential core meltdown. But the procedure required sailors to expose themselves to radioactive gases and steam. The crew's heroic actions successfully averted a meltdown and K-19 was eventually towed back to its base. The accident exposed all of the sub's sailors to higher-than-normal levels of radiation. Eight Soviet crewmen died shortly thereafter from their radiation exposure.

The public record, of course, may represent only a fraction of the deaths, accidents, spills, and contaminations that have happened on nuclear subs, whether at sea or at shipyards undergoing repairs. As writer David B. Kaplan says,

> Despite the many safety problems of civilian reactors, the world's nuclear navies release almost no information on the operation and accident records of these ships. Marine reactors are developed and controlled almost entirely by the world's militaries, with virtually no independent oversight or international control . . . .[accidents], however, are not called "accidents" by the navy. They are "incidents" and "discrepancies." And they are, in the words of the U.S. Atomic Energy Act, "born classified."[28]

▲ The dismantling of decommissioned Russian nuclear submarines, like the two docked here in 1998 at a base in Severomorsk in north-west Russia, has been hampered by lack of funding.

Observers like Kaplan wonder how else than an accident to explain sightings such as the disabled Soviet sub seen being towed back to port at the end of a three-mile-long cable.

The Military's Broken Arrows

Accidents to nuclear submarines' reactors can be compounded by nuclear weapons accidents, which the U.S. military calls "broken arrows." Nuclear bombs, for example, have been on occasion lost or destroyed due to a variety of accidents, including bomb-carrying airplanes crashing, accidentally releasing nuclear weapons over both land and sea, and even, in a 1965 incident, falling off of an aircraft carrier. Bomb-carrying ships and subs that sink have also contributed to a number of nuclear weapons currently lying unrecovered on the floor of the world's oceans. Like Russia and the other members of the nuclear-bomb club, the United States has never been especially open about its broken arrows, though in 1980 it did publish a list of thirty-two nuclear accidents or incidents. The U.S. Department of Defense admits to losing eleven nuclear bombs in accidents and never recovering them. Including other countries' lost weapons, an estimated fifty nuclear warheads lie on the bottom of the world's oceans.

Recovering nuclear weapons lost at sea can be difficult. So can cleaning up the radioactive debris scattered when a nuclear weapon's conventional (nonnuclear) high-explosive trigger detonates. One of the U.S. military's worst broken arrows involved both of these scenarios. On January 17, 1966, a B-52 bomber loaded with four nuclear bombs collided with a tanker plane while attempting a midair refueling off the coast of Spain. The tanker plane exploded, killing all four crew members, and the bomber began to disintegrate. The seven crew members on the bomber had to bail out (four survived). Three of the nuclear weapons landed on the ground in the area of Palomares, a farming community, and one fell into the Mediterranean Sea.

One of the bombs that fell on land was easily found and recovered by the U.S. military. Both of the other bombs that hit the ground, however, had their high-explosive triggers—not their nuclear payloads—detonate on impact. These bombs scattered plutonium and other radioactive material up to five hundred yards away. U.S. officials organized a massive cleanup that eventually required the removal of more than fourteen hundred tons of contaminated soil and vegetation.

◄ This thermonuclear bomb and two others lost in the area of Palomares, Spain, in January 1966, were recovered much more easily than the one that fell into the Mediterranean.

The weapon that fell into the water sank to the seabed floor, almost three thousand feet down. It took a costly three-month search to first locate it, using an Alvin submersible, and then to recover it. According to a Brookings Institution report, "The total cost of the accident—excluding the aircraft, but including the search and decontamination effort and the settlement of more than 500 claims brought by the residents of Palomares—was estimated at more than $120 million." The potential health costs to the Spanish population is unclear. More than one square mile of town and farmland was contaminated, not including surrounding fields that had plutonium dust blown onto them. "Yet there was only sporadic monitoring of villagers and no effort to determine what level of contamination was acceptable,"[29] noted the think-tank report.

Everyday Hazards

Nuclear reactors and nuclear weapons offer enormous accident potential in worst-case scenarios, possibly killing thousands of people and contaminating large swatches of land. Some of the same types of contaminations and malfunctions that have plagued reactors and weapons plants also afflict medical, industrial, and other uses of nuclear technology. Various communities have faced considerable dangers from nuclear materials that have been abandoned, lost, misplaced, or just plain overlooked by regulators. Such incidents do not quite measure up to the doomsday standards of reactor and weapons accidents, but they happen frequently enough to present a real hazard both to the general public and to workers in various nuclear industries.

CHAPTER FOUR

Risky Business

The medical and industrial use of nuclear materials is inherently risky, given that any technology designed to control radiation is subject to failures, exposure to radiation can be difficult to detect, and protective shielding is never perfect. Indeed, just getting the natural resource of uranium out of the ground has been proven to be hazardous. Uranium miners have long been routinely exposed to higher-than-normal levels of radiation, leading to radiation-induced lung cancers. According to the International Physicians for the Prevention of Nuclear War, the largest collective exposure of radiation to workers has been due to uranium mining. "The death rate from lung cancer is five times higher in uranium miners than in the general population,"[30] a report in the *Lancet* notes.

Disaster at Church Rock

The aftermath of uranium mining also has its hazards. One of the most dramatic mining-related nuclear disasters occurred outside the small town of Church Rock in northwestern New Mexico only a few months after Three Mile Island. It caused what one scientist has termed "the largest release (by volume) of low-level radioactive waste in U.S. history."[31] On the morning of July 16, 1979, a twenty-five-foot-high earthen dam built by Virginia-based United Nuclear Corporation (UNC) failed. The dam was holding back more than one thousand tons of solid waste and almost 100 million gallons of liquid waste resulting from the operation of an underground uranium mine. The flood of hazardous radioactive materials spilled into the nearby Rio Puerco and rushed south, contaminating tribal grounds of the local Navajo and backing up sewers twenty miles downstream. Hazardous levels of radioactivity and

A DEADLY GLOW

Beginning in the 1920s, a number of clock making companies began to offer glow-in-the-dark products. Watch dials, clock faces, automobile dashboard gauges, and airplane instrument panels were made luminescent by adding the radioactive element radium to paint. To fashion neat numbers, the mostly young women who worked in these factories were encouraged to occasionally "sharpen" their brushes with their lips and teeth. The workers were thus ingesting deadly radium. Years later these women experienced a high incidence of jawbone deterioration and fatal cancers of the head and neck. Researchers have studied their lives to learn more about the long-term health effects of radiation exposure.

Ross Mullner, author of *Deadly Glow: The Radium Dial Worker Tragedy*, notes that the federal government passed a number of safety regulations in the aftermath of these accidental radium exposures. Occupational laws now protect workers involved in various aspects of the nuclear industry, from nuclear power to waste management.

▲ In July 1998, two women look over a map identifying areas of Ottawa, Illinois, that suffered radioactive contamination from the activities of the now-defunct Radium Dial Company.

heavy-metal contamination were later detected in the local groundwater as the flood traveled downstream into Arizona before dissipating.

The tailings spill could be traced to multiple causes. UNC was operating the waste pond for six months beyond its eighteen-month design life and had allowed the waste level to crest two feet higher than called for in the dam design. Government investigators later determined that the dam was located over an unstable geologic formation and that cracks had developed that should have warned the company of an imminent failure.

Company and government efforts to clean up the spill could not prevent the vast majority of the radioactive waste from soaking into the earth, threatening nearby aquifers, and lingering in the food chain for years. Water samples taken from local streams conducted as late as 1987 confirmed the continued presence of higher-than-normal concentrations of radioactivity. Although researchers have never documented any adverse health effects directly caused by the accident, extra cancers may have resulted over the years. Within a year UNC had built a (presumably stronger) dam and started a new waste pond. The mine closed in 1982 but the tailings site remains in need of cleanup to this day. Local officials say that the current rock cover on the tailings pile shows signs of premature deterioration.

Medical Mishaps

Soon after the discovery of radioactivity and X rays in the 1890s, medical doctors were exploiting the new properties to both diagnose and treat patients. Telephone inventor Alexander Graham Bell was a notable contributor to the field in 1903, being among the first to suggest placing a source of radium near bodily tumors to kill cancer cells. By the 1930s medical technicians had machines that could generate "artificial radioactivity" to treat leukemia and other conditions. A landmark advance occurred in 1946 when doctors found that radioactive iodine could target and wipe out cancer in the thyroid gland. Advances have accumulated with technological and computer breakthroughs over the past decade.

Doctors now can use almost one hundred different nuclear medicine procedures, from simple diagnostic X rays to the so-called Gamma Knife that focuses gamma rays from a radioactive substance such as cobalt-60 on specific locations in the body. Countless patients have benefited from the use of relatively small amounts of radioactive materials to identify or kill cancer cells. On the other hand, radiation therapy is a complex nuclear technology involving numerous professionals and dozens of sessions using high-tech equipment. Radiology and nuclear medicine thus have experienced their share of accidents and mishaps. According to the U.S. Radiation Accident Registry database, of the thirty people who died as the result of nuclear accidents from 1944 to 2000, twenty-two were killed by mishaps during either radiation therapy or nuclear medicine. Says principal author Robert C. Ricks:

> These accidents in hospitals and other medical facilities occurred because of classical errors: wrong patient, wrong dosage (for example, mistaking "milli" for "micro"), wrong medication or because of irradiation of the wrong area of the body. Other errors resulting in injury or death included failure to determine if a female was pregnant or nursing, incorrect calibration of therapy devices, incorrect computer programming, errors in equipment maintenance or repair, negligence, and malpractice.[32]

Two of the most deadly nuclear medicine accidents have happened within the past decade in Central America. In 1996 in Costa Rica, an erroneously calibrated cobalt-60 therapy unit was used on hundreds of patients. Estimates of the number of deaths from the radiation overdoses range from seven to forty-five. The most recent radiological accident occurred at a cancer institute in Panama, where some thirty patients were injured and at least six killed. The problem was traced to a fault in the computer program used to run the irradiation machine. Similar accidents appear to be increasing as high-tech radiation therapy machines become more widespread. A review article on radiation accidents worldwide published in 2001 concluded that "accidents with radiation devices have become more frequent since 1970, reaching 40-45 events per five-year periods."[33]

Cesium Unleashed on Goiania

Radiation therapy machines can also cause accidents when, for various reasons, their radioactive materials inadvertently are released into the environment. Even tiny amounts of the cobalt, cesium, or other elements found in these machines can cause harmful health effects, so the improper disposal of a medical radiation machine can cause a serious accident that affects not just one person but a whole community.

One of the most notorious such incidents occurred in September 1987 when residents of Goiania, a city of seven hundred thousand in central Brazil, took apart a cancer therapy machine that contained a matchbox-sized, twenty-gram supply of radioactive cesium-137. Cesium is especially disastrous as a substance to unleash upon the public, since it emits difficult-to-block gamma radiation and easily combines with other elements that can be taken up by the human body. "In a nuclear disaster second only to Chernobyl," says reporter Alex Neifert, "the city of Goiania had one of the largest radioactive leaks on its hands and for a few days, they knew nothing about it."[34]

The machine ultimately responsible for the Goiania accident was left behind in an abandoned cancer clinic. Scavengers found the canister containing cesium-137 and managed to pry it open. The cake of luminous blue powder was a novelty. One six-year-old girl rubbed the sparkling substance onto her face. Adults passed the material on to friends and family, a number of whom also rubbed it on their bodies or put a small piece in their pockets. It was a week before

▼ Workers prepare an abandoned quarry in Goiania for the disposal of radioactive waste generated during the 1987 contamination episode. The quarry was filled in and covered over to make a large park.

health care workers correctly diagnosed some of the painful burns that these people began to experience as radiation injuries. By then the cesium-137 had begun to contaminate vehicles, homes, and businesses. Ambulances that picked up people with the cesium-137 on their bodies and clothing also became contaminated, spreading the toxin to pregnant women and others who later rode in the same vehicles.

Closing Pandora's Box

The Brazilian government asked the IAEA for help and the agency responded by sending a team of experts with experience in radiation accidents. They identified 249 contaminated people, including twenty who were internally contaminated—"The patients themselves were radioactive,"[35] noted a report in *Science*. Even with medical treatment, four of the people, including the six-year-old girl, died from the radiation within a week. They had to be buried in lead-lined coffins and concrete graves. A major cleanup collected contaminated clothing, furniture, dirt, and other materials. Two houses needed to be encased in concrete and dozens more destroyed or abandoned. Many other town residents may have suffered from radiation-linked cancer in subsequent years.

In the United States, the NRC says that it receives about three hundred reports every year relating to lost or stolen radioactive materials. The IAEA notes that it has documented almost four hundred cases of illegal sales of nuclear materials since 1993. Regulatory control of cancer machines and the like may be especially lax in countries such as Brazil, according to Neifert's case study of the Goiania incident:

> The best protection one can have against a large-scale nuclear disaster happening is two-fold: better regulation and better preparation. The lack of adequate response time and materials greatly contributed to the number of casualties and fatalities. Although it took a few days to report the radioactive leakage, the cause is also twofold. Primarily, the canister should never have been left behind. Secondly, the general public had no idea that they were handling a radioactive substance. The lack of regulation of nuclear substances, whether for medical purposes or electricity, remains a major factor in the possibility of future nuclear accidents.[36]

Radioactive material lost or stolen from medical or industrial nuclear technology can also be used maliciously. The

THE RADIOACTIVE BOY SCOUT

On June 26, 1995, officials from the U.S. Environmental Protection Agency descended on a shed behind a suburban house in a small Michigan town for an unusual job: They had to cart off the dangerously radioactive materials that teenager David Hahn had fashioned during his extended experiments with nuclear technology. Inspired by his Boy Scout merit badge in atomic energy, Hahn had attempted to build a primitive nuclear reactor. A reactor turned out to be beyond Hahn's reach, but he did manage to make a nuclear mixture that started to become increasingly radioactive each day.

In order to conduct his nuclear experiments, Hahn decided he needed two things. One was technical nuclear information, some of which he got in phone calls to unsuspecting officials at the NRC. The other was a significant amount of radioactive materials. He was able to obtain these from sources such as broken smoke detectors (a source of americium-241); clocks with luminous dials (radium-226); the nat-ural mineral pitchblende (uranium-238 and -235); and Coleman-style gas lantern mantles (thorium-232).

Hahn's backyard experiments with these nuclear materials soon threatened to turn his suburban neighborhood into a nuclear waste site. He was caught only after he had dismantled the experiment, fearing the growing radiation he was exposing himself and even neighbors to. Most of the radioactive materials went into the garbage but a traffic stop led to police finding some in the trunk of his car. David calmly told them it was not an atomic bomb but it was radioactive. This led to the calling in of the FBI and to moon-suited EPA technicians coming to cut up his shed and cart it off to a nuclear waste site.

"These are conditions that regulatory agencies never envision," EPA official David Minnaar told *Harper's Magazine*. "It's simply presumed that the average person wouldn't have the technology or materials required to experiment in these areas."

most notorious example of this occurred in November 1995, when rebels from the Russian region of Chechnya seized a hospital and took more than thirty pounds of cesium from cancer radiation equipment. They put the cesium, along with some dynamite, in a container and buried it near the entrance to a popular park in Moscow. Since authorities discovered the "dirty bomb" before it could be detonated, it probably did more harm to its makers than to anyone else.

Lost Generators and Lethal Lighthouses

Political unrest in parts of the former Soviet Union over the past decade may have also contributed to accidents involving some unusual types of abandoned nuclear technology. In 2001 two people were trying to salvage scrap metal from a lighthouse situated in a remote area along Russia's northern coast. They inadvertently exposed themselves to radiation when they came across the facility's nuclear-powered generator. Later that year a pair of lumberjacks in the western Georgia region of the former Soviet Union suffered severe radiation sickness and burns when they stumbled across a similar nuclear-powered generator left behind by the Soviet military.

These forgotten but still hazardous pieces of technology are so-called "radioisotope thermoelectric generators" (RTGs). Much simpler than nuclear reactors, they use the heat generated by the decay of strontium, plutonium, or other radioactive materials to make electricity. Similar radiation-powered thermoelectric generators have been used for various other applications, such as to power weather stations and space satellites.

Since the mid-1960s Russia has built more than 130 lighthouses that use strontium-containing RTGs to produce electricity to power the lighthouses' lamps. Russia admits that the unmanned lighthouses are slipping through the cracks and may pose an environmental threat. According to writer Thomas Nilsen, Russian nuclear specialists inspected lighthouses in Siberia in 2002 and described most of them as being in terrible condition:

The radiation levels near the lighthouses exceeded the permitted level, which indicates the possibility of radioactive leakage. But the scariest thing was that the inspectors have not found all the lighthouses they were looking for. There is a slim chance they were stolen and a big chance that the Russian authorities simply lack the full overview of the lighthouses' locations.[37]

Due to worries that terrorists could steal the strontium from the un-

IRRADIATED PACIFIERS

In the United States the irradiation industry treats mostly medical products, household products such as bandages and baby pacifiers, and a few foods, particularly spices. Other countries such as China and South Africa now irradiate a wider range of foods. The irradiation industry in the United States has been actively seeking to expand its market by processing more foods and other products. Since 1986 the Food and Drug Administration and the Department of Agriculture have approved the use of irradiation on fruits and vegetables, wheat flour, poultry, and meat. Many consumers have resisted the technology as inappropriate, or even hazardous, for foods. After the anthrax scare in early 2002, the U.S. government began to irradiate mail bound for Congress and federal agencies at postal facilities outside of Washington, so mail may soon join food as potential selling points for the irradiation industry.

guarded lighthouses or abandoned military generators and use it to build a "dirty bomb" like the one found in the Moscow park, the IAEA has begun to help Russia find and dismantle its lost nuclear-powered lighthouses. It is quite practical to change the energy source in these lighthouses to a combination of solar and battery power.

Irradiation Facility Foul-Ups

Worldwide there are now some 170 industrial irradiation facilities that sterilize foods, disposable medical and pharmaceutical supplies, and other products by briefly exposing them to a microorganism-killing radioactive substance. This technology is subject to the same safety considerations—and accidents—as other nuclear technologies. Thus, there have been dozens of incidents of radioactive material spilled inside and outside irradiation facilities, nuclear material lost in transit, and workers exposed to harmful levels of radiation.

A notable incident occurred at an irradiation facility near the Central American city of San Salvador, El Salvador. The plant sterilized medical products using a cobalt-60 source. On February 5, 1989, the plant's moving belt got stuck. Three workers managed to bypass safety systems and enter the radiation room. They got the belt moving again but also exposed themselves to doses of radiation high enough to develop acute radiation sickness. Even with specialized hospital treatment over the next few months, two of the men had to have their legs and feet amputated. The other man died from his radiation injuries about six months after the accident.

Such serious injuries and fatalities are relatively rare occurrences at irradiation plants. It is much more common for irradiation facilities to experience contamination accidents due to spills during the shipping, handling, and disposing of nuclear products and wastes. The Nuclear Regulatory Commission says that there have been at least fifty-four accidents at irradiation facilities worldwide since 1974. Companies have been known to illegally bypass regulatory requirements to meet production schedules, or to hire low-paid, poorly trained workers. Other irradiators have been caught throwing radioactive wastes out with the trash or flushing it down the toilet. In 1988, an irradiator in Decatur, Georgia, experienced a leak of cesium-137 into the water

▲ In April 1997, a technician checks for radiation at the side of a truck bearing the concrete-encased reactor vessel from the shutdown Yankee Rowe nuclear plant in western Massachusetts. The nuclear waste is being transported to a burial site in South Carolina.

storage pool in the radiation room. Workers inadvertently spread contamination from the plant into their cars, homes, and local community. Taxpayers paid for the $30 million cleanup.

A Future of "Mobile Chernobyls"?

The radioactive materials needed for radiation therapy machines, food irradiation facilities, and various industrial uses all need to be transported from producers to users. An estimated 10 million radioactive packages are now transported throughout the world—including approximately 3 million packages of radioactive material shipped in the United States—every year by road, rail, air, and sea.

Accidents during this nuclear commerce promote public jitters. In January 2002, a Swedish company shipped radioactive iridium-192 by Federal Express from Sweden to New Orleans, with stops in Paris and Memphis. When the steel container registered an alarming level of radiation leakage at its destination, technicians opened it by remote control. Radioactive pellets had spilled out of two of the three capsules enclosed within an iron envelope. A FedEx representative estimated that as many as sixty people may have come into close contact with the container and been exposed to high levels of radiation.

The shipping of radioactive waste represents another threat. From 1949 until 1996, there were seventy-two reported accidents involving radioactive waste shipments, according to the Washington, D.C.–based Environmental Working Group, authors of a detailed study on nuclear transit accidents. "In four cases," they say, "there was accidental radioactive material contamination beyond the transport vehicle, in four more there was accidental radioactive material contamination that was confined to the vehicle. There were 13 incidents or traffic accidents that resulted in no release or contamination, and 49 incidents of accidental surface contamination that required clean up."[38]

A recent example involved a double tractor-trailer. Traveling on Interstate 65 south of Nashville, Tennessee, it hit a bridge and guardrail. The truck overturned and spilled its load of low-level radioactive medical waste on the roadway. Because the waste was not highly radioactive, officials were able to clean up the mess and reopen the road within eight hours.

For environmentalists who are opposing the federal government's plans for shipping seventy thousand tons of

 ## REACTORS FALLING FROM THE SKY

The Russians have been more aggressive than the United States in sending nuclear reactors into space, having launched thirty-one between 1967 and 1988. The three reactor accidents the Russian space program has experienced have probably caused much more environmental contamination than any RTG incident. One of the reactor accidents occurred during a launch failure and two when reactor-powered radar satellites were not boosted to suitable orbits. The reactor aboard Kosmos 954 contaminated a broad area of Canada's Northwest Territories when it burned up on reentry in 1978. Kosmos 1402 suffered a similar fate after it was launched in late 1982. According to NASA, "The reactor core separated from the remainder of the spacecraft and was the last piece of the satellite to return to Earth in February 1983. The reactor core returned in the South Atlantic Ocean, leaving a radioactive trail through the atmosphere."

▲ An experimental nuclear rocket engine makes a late evening arrival at a test stand in Jackass Flats, Nevada, in December 1967.

radioactive waste from around the country to a Nevada depository, the accident was a troubling indication of future "mobile Chernobyls." Transportation opponents note that spent nuclear fuel removed from a reactor's core is still highly radioactive, and that even the latest high-tech shipping containers cannot prevent waste handlers, drivers, and the general public from being exposed to radiation during routine (non-accident) conditions.

Nuclear Accidents in Space

Nuclear materials are transported not only on Earth but also into space. The American and Russian space programs have well established nuclear power projects. The National Aeronautics and Space Administration (NASA) says that since 1961 the United States has launched two dozen spacecraft carrying some significant level of radioactive material. All but one of the American launches carried low-power radioisotope thermoelectric generators, like those found in Russia's forgotten lighthouses. The RTGs were used to power experiments aboard *Pioneer*, *Voyager*, and other spacecraft sent to explore the outer planets. Space missions have also left RTG-powered rovers on the Moon and Mars. NASA last launched a nuclear-powered spacecraft, *Cassini*, in 1997. Its RTG was fueled by seventy-three pounds of plutonium.

The United States did launch one small nuclear reactor into space, in April 1965. The reactor stopped working after about six weeks but remains in an orbit that, NASA says, will allow its radioactive materials to decay to a safe level before it falls to Earth in three thousand years.

America's nuclear space program has had a few mission failures leading to environmental contamination from space-craft with RTGs aboard. (The reactor-powered satellites are launched using conventional chemical-propelled rockets; American scientists developed experimental nuclear-propelled rockets during the 1960s but NASA canceled the program in 1971.) The most serious accident occurred after the launch of Space Nuclear Auxiliary Power (SNAP) 9-A on April 21, 1964. A Department of Defense weather satellite, SNAP 9-A failed to achieve its correct orbit and dispersed its

▼ Technicians at Cape Canaveral, Florida, install a plutonium-bearing RTG on the *Cassini* spacecraft prior to its October 1997 launch.

nuclear fuel into the upper atmosphere while burning up upon returning to Earth. Scientists from the Atomic Energy Commission were able to measure the resulting radioactive contamination in both air and soil samples.

Post-Disaster Hazards

Despite well-intentioned safety plans and dedicated personnel, accidents in space as well as on the ground, at nuclear power plants, irradiation facilities, and industrial sites, can lead to unavoidable consequences, including injuries and deaths to plant operators or to the general public. Unlike many other disasters, the rescue and cleanup work can be just as hazardous as the disaster itself, especially for the firefighters, doctors, and plant officials at the site of the accident.

CHAPTER FIVE

Nuclear 911: Rescue and Response

What many nuclear disasters have in common is a challenging post-accident scenario that requires expert personnel to perform hazardous rescue and cleanup work. Investigating the causes of a nuclear accident can be a difficult, expensive, and time-consuming job. Many investigations involve multiple agencies and hundreds of researchers, and may take years to complete. Investigators' findings, however, often prove to be well worth the effort since they can suggest important safety reforms.

From Firefighters to Doctors

Dozens of emergency workers were among the first to the scene of the Chernobyl accident. Firefighters climbed to the roof of the reactor building to battle multiple fires that threatened to spread to a nearby reactor. Helicopter pilots flew mission after mission, dumping tons of sand, lead, and firefighting chemicals on the blaze. While the initial violent explosion at Chernobyl killed two plant operators, acute radiation sickness over the next days and weeks claimed the lives of another twenty-nine firefighters and emergency workers. "They were just ordinary people who became heroes within a minute, when they sacrificed their lives, saving millions of people,"[39] said Chernobyl station commander Oleg Orlov.

In addition to firefighters and emergency cleanup workers, among those first to be called to help cope with a nuclear

▲ A woman holds a portrait of her husband who died after he helped with the cleanup of the Chernobyl explosion, during an April 2002 memorial ceremony in Kiev.

accident are government agencies and civil defense officials. Countries with nuclear facilities have developed detailed plans for coping with nuclear emergencies, whether low-level incidents or more serious accidents. In the United States the facility's private owner, local and state governments, and the main federal agency for the industry, the NRC, coordinate these plans. International agencies like the IAEA have become more involved in the most serious accidents since Chernobyl.

Doctors, nurses, and public health experts are also included among emergency teams after a nuclear accident. For example, the Chernobyl firefighters who had been exposed to massive doses of radiation were quickly airlifted from nearby Kiev to Moscow's Hospital No. 6, the site of the country's top radiation-treatment clinic. More than two hundred persons at Chernobyl needed immediate hospitalization for acute radiation sickness. Chief radiologist Angelina Guskova, one of the most prominent radiation injury specialists in the world, was soon directing the treatments, such as emergency bone marrow transplants, that offered the workers the only chance for survival.

The treatments conducted by Guskova and others at the Moscow clinic, including American volunteers such as the noted physician Robert Gale, helped to save numerous lives. "There's still no overestimating the importance of this first stage of work, because with radiation sickness you can't delay,"[40] she told *Chernobyl* author Andrey Illesh. All of the firefighters who worked closest to the accident, however, eventually succumbed—some had received radiation doses that were estimated to be four times the fatal dose.

Tools of the Trade

The high levels of radiation at the Chernobyl disaster site presented unusual hazards for first responders. The possibility of spreading contamination means that even the transport of exposed victims must be approached with caution, as was seen with the contamination of ambulances in the Goiania incident in 1987. When accidents do not result in significant releases of radiation into the environment, however, emergency medical and cleanup personnel often still face serious problems requiring specially designed tools and cautious procedures.

After some of the earliest nuclear accidents, first-response personnel often found themselves donning raincoats and gloves and hoping for the best. Radiation accident response has become a more technical and specialized field in recent years. In the United States, graduate-level college courses in the field have been developed with guidance from the Department of Energy's Radiation Emergency Assistance Center/Training Site. Specialists study the fundamentals of nuclear physics, diagnosis of acute radiation exposure, and how to detect and measure radiation.

When an accident does occur, depending upon its seriousness, trained federal, state, and local teams may be dispatched to the scene. Emergency responders' immediate concerns are to secure the area. This is much easier if, for example, the accident is inside a nuclear power plant than if it is

ON THE CHERNOBYL FRONT LINE: RUSSIAN DOCTOR ANGELINA GUSKOVA

Angelina Guskova was well trained and prepared for the crucial role she played in saving the lives of people exposed to Chernobyl's radiation. She had followed family members from three previous generations into medicine. Her 1985 book, *The Organization of Observations of Workers in the Nuclear Industry*, contained a chapter with guidelines on how to organize aid to the victims of a nuclear reactor accident.

Guskova has remained a prominent medical specialist and researcher on the aftereffects of Chernobyl, up to and beyond the celebration of her seventy-fifth birthday in 1999. She is one of the three authors of the encyclopedic *Medical Management of Radiation Accidents*, published in 2001 by CRC Press of Boca Raton, Florida. Lately Guskova has been encouraged by her studies that indicate Chernobyl has caused relatively few long-term injuries to the general populace. On the other hand, she notes, psychological factors and a widespread "victim's complex" have led to persistent social problems.

a spill of radioactive material on a public highway. In the latter case emergency response teams may use special remote-control warning signs and boundary designators to direct traffic and keep the public away. First responders also need to prevent the spread of contamination, reduce any further radiation exposure to victims and to rescue personnel, and offer emergency medical treatment. Hospitals with personnel who are knowledgeable about treating radiation victims will be notified.

Rescue personnel may wear special protective clothing, including disposable coveralls, hoods, and boots to protect against radioactive dust. Heavier-duty rubber suits, lead-impregnated safety glasses and face shields, and specialized sleeves, aprons, and barriers can also be used during emergencies. In Japan, after the accident that killed two men at the nuclear fuel processing facility in Tokaimura, it became national policy to distribute radiation protection outfits to police headquarters in localities with nuclear facilities.

The Hit-and-Run Response

Although the techniques as well as the equipment used in nuclear accident cleanups have become more sophisticated, the options for dealing with radioactive materials are still somewhat limited. Nuclear materials can be so toxic that, if the concentration is high enough, the only viable approach is to smother or entomb them. These actions can be dangerous, of course, since workers have been known to suffer great harm during nuclear cleanup or rescue. The six hundred thousand Russian cleanup workers—the so-called "liquidators"—who dealt with the mess at Chernobyl have since been shown to have suffered from high rates of cancer.

The experience of one early Canadian cleanup worker has no doubt been mirrored many times since. In the mid-1950s, Bjarnie Hannibal Paulson was a Korean War vet, a corporal in the Royal Canadian Air Force, and an instructor in Atomic Warfare and Radioactive Decontamination. His courage and expertise were badly needed on May 24, 1958, when a nuclear accident occurred at a reactor at the National Research Universal (NRU) reactor in Ontario. Reactor operators controlling a robotic crane were removing uranium fuel rods that had overheated or, in one case, caught on fire. One three-foot-long rod slipped from the robot's grasp and dropped to the floor in

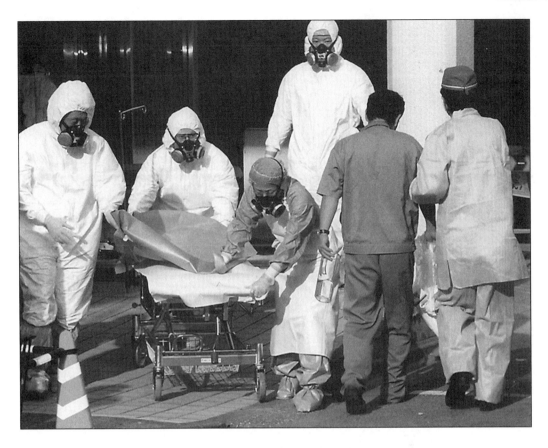

▲ Japanese rescue personnel wear protective clothing and breathing devices at the 1999 Tokaimura accident.

a maintenance area. Because the reactor building's ventilation system was open, radiation began spreading throughout the building and even escaping into the environment.

Authorities quickly organized more than six hundred army recruits and other men for an emergency action. Paulson helped to outfit the men with protective clothing and respirators and to organize them into groups of fifteen. The teams took turns sprinting past the area with the burning uranium fuel, stopping only long enough to dump a bucket of wet sand on the fire. The men could not linger because the radioactivity was so intense. This hit-and-run tactic has had to be used often enough that the nuclear industry has various names, such as "jumpers" and "glow boys," for the often-underpaid young men who are willing to do it. The relay cleanup eventually started to cool the fire. Paulson then helped to wash radioactive particles off the cleanup crew itself.

A half-dozen years later Paulson first began to wonder whether his efforts at the NRU accident had caused long-term damage to his health. He gradually found his strength and sense of vitality leaking away. This was shortly before he underwent the first of what would be more than forty operations for cancer over the next fifteen years. He believes that the cancers were the direct result of exposure he suffered during the cleanup to alpha particles that got lodged in the hair follicles of his body. He has since experienced great difficulty in getting the Canadian government to cover his injury and acknowledge the danger many similar rescue workers faced.

Atomic Energy of Canada Limited (AECL) has steadfastly maintained that workers like Paulson were exposed to only low levels of radiation. It also rejects claims that exposures could have caused any adverse health effects. As accident writer Jim Green has observed:

> The methodology for this second conclusion appears to have been the ostrich technique: no follow-up studies were carried out, the men involved in the clean-up were told to observe strict secrecy about the operation, claims that adverse health effects were linked to the clean-up were vigorously denied, and AECL has refused to supply information that would assist in the location of men involved in the clean-up and thus facilitate follow-up studies.[41]

Rocky Times at Rocky Flats

Cleaning up nuclear accidents can be costly in economic as well as health terms. The U.S. government has estimated that it may have to spend up to $350 billion to clean up the accidents and routine pollution from its nuclear weapons factories alone over the next seventy-five years. Many of the hundred or so facilities have contaminated equipment and buildings, storage tanks and pools that are leaking radioactive wastes, and underground radioactive plumes creeping toward population centers.

One of America's most polluted and accident-prone nuclear sites was Rocky Flats, which was established outside Denver in 1951 to help manufacture nuclear warheads. The environmental group Clamshell Alliance says that Rocky Flats experienced at least 271 fires and 410 contamination incidents before its nuclear activities ended in 1989. Perhaps the most devastating accident was the September 1957 fire that released plutonium-laden smoke that drifted over metropolitan areas of Denver. (Federal officials did not bother to inform

either the public or the Colorado state government about the plutonium release.) A similar fire twelve years later caused much less offsite radiation exposure but posed a tougher cleanup challenge.

▲ Cleanup personnel deal with the mess created by the 1969 fire at Colorado's Rocky Flats nuclear weapons plant.

Just before 2:30 on the Sunday afternoon of May 11, 1969, plutonium, which is naturally flammable, being kept in an open can within a glovebox caught on fire. (Gloveboxes are enclosed containers that workers can reach into through holes fitted with protective rubber gloves, thus allowing them to handle highly radioactive materials.) The fire soon spread throughout much of Building 776 as other gloveboxes, which shared a ventilation system, and wood fiber and plastic shielding caught on fire. It took firefighters almost six hours to contain the blaze. The building's filtration system caught "essentially all of the plutonium" in the smoke before it could be dispersed into the air and spread downwind, according to a five-volume AEC report. The report noted, however, that one firefighter received "a significant internal body burden of plutonium" and that "the building was grossly contaminated with plutonium."[42] Furthermore, plutonium "was tracked out of Building 776 by the firefighters and was detectable on the ground beyond the building."[43]

The building's inadequate fire-prevention measures led to one of the most costly industrial accidents in U.S. history—the cleanup tab reached $50 million. In the ensuing months massive amounts of radioactive materials had to be shipped in railway cars to a waste storage site in Idaho. The accident's legacy lives on there—wastes from the fire that were illegally dumped in trenches are now threatening to contaminate a huge underground reservoir that supplies drinking water for much of the Northwest.

Since its closure in the early 1990s Rocky Flats has been the site of one of the most ambitious nuclear cleanup efforts anywhere. The Department of Energy expects to pay more than $7 billion to clean up 170 areas of suspected contamination on the site by 2010. Contractors must dismantle, deactivate, or decommission more than one hundred tons of plutonium-bearing leftovers.

Burying Russia's Radioactive Lake

Russia is similarly challenged by its nuclear past. The Chelyabinsk areas are probably even more contaminated than Hanford or Rocky Flats. So much radioactive material has been dumped into Russia's Lake Karachai—the one that had contaminated a broad area when it dried up in 1967 and high winds distributed radioactive particles far and wide—that it has come to be recognized as perhaps the most polluted spot on Earth.

Karachai is an example of a cleanup action alleviating one type of threat only to cause another. By the late 1990s, the lake had regained its previous water levels. It had also regained any radioactivity lost in the 1967 disaster—and then some. Karachai was thought to contain as much radiation as released during the Chernobyl accident. Scientists said that just standing on its shore for a matter of minutes could expose an individual to a fatal dose of radiation.

To prevent the type of atmospheric dispersal that occurred in 1967, within recent years the Russians have begun to fill the lake with large concrete cylinders. Unfortunately, filling up the lake, which is located within the watershed between two river valleys, is driving the hazardous radioactive materials into the ground beneath the lake. Observational wells in the area have confirmed that lake solutions leaking into the local aquifer contain radioactive strontium, cesium,

IODINE TO THE RESCUE

Taking supplements of the mineral potassium iodide immediately prior to exposure to fallout containing radioactive iodine may provide an important health benefit to the thyroid gland. Chernobyl researchers have found a dramatic increase in thyroid cancers among those exposed to radioactive iodine following the accident. Potassium iodide works by blocking the thyroid's ability to absorb radioactive iodine. It needs to be taken within twenty-four hours of exposure to be effective. Potassium iodide, however, does not protect against other types of radiation—nor does any other supplement. A dozen U.S. states and a number of European countries have within recent years passed out supplies of potassium iodide tablets to populations that live near nuclear power plants and other nuclear facilities.

▲ Government programs to hand out potassium iodide (KI) are sometimes protested as a distraction from the issue of nuclear power plant safety. This man is protesting a KI program at New York's Indian Point nuclear power plant.

cobalt, uranium, and plutonium. Russian officials now face a new threat as this underground plume of radioactive groundwater moves toward a river a mile away.

The plume is advancing at a rate of about three feet per day. If the plume reaches Siberian river systems, "Western Siberia and the Arctic Ocean will be polluted with radioactive waste, triggering a global disaster within ten years, where international intervention may be required," according to Yuri Vishnevsky, a Russian nuclear official. "No technology is available now to keep the plume in place,"[44] he says.

Mexico's El Cobalto

Response and cleanup crews sometimes face public health dangers much more immediate than ten years down the line. This was the case in December 1983, when a twenty-year-old radiation therapy machine ended up abandoned in a Juarez, Mexico, warehouse. Handyman Vincente Sotelo, while transporting the device to a junkyard, took an unmarked capsule from the machine. Upon later prying it open, he found that it contained more than six thousand tiny pellets of radioactive cobalt-60. Some of these pellets spilled out to contaminate Sotelo's pickup truck and then local streets. Other pellets remained in the capsule while it was sold as scrap, mixed with metals, and shipped to two Mexican foundries. One foundry thus inadvertently made radioactive metal table legs and the other radioactive steel reinforcement rods ("rebar").

It was more than a month later before a truck carrying some of the contaminated rebar made a wrong turn near the entrance to New Mexico's Los Alamos National Laboratory, the nuclear research facility. When the truck set off radiation alarms, American and Mexican authorities began to piece together the sequence of events. The cobalt in the bars was traced back to the junkyard, Sotelo's pickup (which triggered Geiger counters from three hundred yards away), and the abandoned radiation machine.

Officials faced a nightmare trying to locate all of the radioactive pellets, table legs, and rebar. More than one hundred homes and buildings in Mexico and the southern United States that had been built with the rebar had to be torn down. Extensive searches with radiation detectors found pellets stuck in roads and scattered elsewhere in the Juarez area. Unknown numbers of pellets remain unaccounted for, threatening to shower any person unfortunate to pick them up with a ra-

DETECTING THE INVISIBLE THREAT

Emergency responders use a number of technologies to monitor radiation exposure, both to themselves and to others at the scene. Rescue personnel typically wear dosimeters or film badges, small devices that can record cumulative exposure to some types of radiation. In some instances technicians may have mechanical devices for measuring radiological contamination, such as a Geiger counter. Developed by the German physicist Hans Geiger (1882–1945), these easy-to-use machines can detect different types of ionizing radiation, such as alpha and beta particles as well as gamma rays, depending upon calibration. In serious accidents, response teams may also have even more sophisticated radiation detection devices, such as those capable of detecting neutrons or providing detailed dosage rates. First responders need to keep track of their personal exposure because the U.S. government has developed guidelines that limit emergency responders' exposure. A person saving lives is allowed a higher exposure than someone who is merely protecting property.

▲ Mobile monitoring devices, like the portable air sampler being held by a technician, and the two instruments in the foreground for measuring radiation, are vital tools for emergency response.

diation dose of about twenty-five rads per hour. Finding, cleaning up, and burying all of the contaminated products ultimately cost more than $30 million.

The Juarez incident exposed junkyard workers and hundreds of other people to potentially harmful levels of radiation. Somewhat surprisingly, Sotelo seemed to have escaped at least immediate injury. He did get arrested for theft, however, and held in prison, where the guards dubbed him El Cobalto—the Cobalt Man.

Beyond "Duck and Cover"

Juarez was a stealth nuclear incident—undetected while much of its harm was being done—but Three Mile Island and other accidents are typical of those accompanied by public announcements and evacuation plans. Nuclear emergency guidelines are now more detailed than the government slogan to "duck and cover" (jump under a desk and put hands over head) familiar to children who attended elementary school during the late 1950s. While that may well be as effective as any tactic in surviving an atomic bomb attack, government agencies have since developed new guidelines for how to survive various types of nuclear accidents.

The U.S. Federal Emergency Management Agency (FEMA), which coordinates national response to disasters, notes that three main factors affect an individual's radiation exposure: distance, shielding, and time. To keep exposure to a minimum, therefore, a person should try to move away from the source of radiation. (In certain circumstances, people who live near but not in the immediate area of a nuclear accident

▼ Duck and cover, shown here being done by schoolchildren in St. Petersburg, Florida, was a routine drill during the early 1960s, when public anxiety peaked over the possibility of nuclear war.

may be best off by staying home and "sheltering in place" rather than evacuating, so it is best to wait until local officials recommend a general evacuation.) Also, individuals should keep heavy, dense materials between themselves and the source of the radiation. This means stay indoors, and limit the duration of being in the vicinity of the accident.

FEMA also recommends keeping crucial disaster supplies on hand, such as flashlight, battery-operated radio, extra batteries, a first-aid kit and manual, emergency food and water. If government officials advise staying at home, people should also close and lock windows, doors, and fireplace dampers, and turn off air conditioning, vents, fans, and furnace. Officials recommend staying in a basement or other underground area until authorities say it is safe.

Such grim emergency scenarios underscore the importance of reducing the likelihood of nuclear accidents and preventing the worst type from ever happening.

CHAPTER SIX

The Challenge of Preventing Nuclear Accidents

A number of reforms in the electric power and other nuclear industries in recent years have focused on improving safety and increasing the number of precautions in place. The early history of the nuclear industry was fraught with government cover-ups of accidents and downplaying of hazards. Operators at a Swedish nuclear plant who noticed high levels of radiation on their monitors on April 28, 1986, and immediately began checking their own facility for leaks, did not learn until twelve hours later that the radiation was coming from an accident that had begun two days earlier at the Chernobyl plant in the Soviet Union. In recent years the public has become better informed about accidents and many governments have become more proactive in instituting stringent safety measures in response to lessons learned.

Chernobyl was undeniably a disaster but if it had one beneficial effect it was to underscore the importance of safety and to demonstrate the potential for harm when nuclear accidents happen. Nuclear reactors are increasingly regulated by government bodies that are not also charged with promoting nuclear energy, a conflict of interest that shortchanged safety in the past. (The United States separated the two functions when Congress abolished the AEC and created the NRC in 1974.) Plants have been designed with an abundance of built-in safety features to reduce the likelihood of accidents—so many, in fact, that safety systems account for about one-quarter of the cost of building a nuclear power reactor.

Nevertheless thirteen Chernobyl-style nuclear reactors still operate in Russia and Lithuania. International agencies have helped these countries make a number of changes to the facilities' design and operation to reduce the likelihood of another top-level disaster. "However, safety concerns remain," according to the IAEA, "particularly regarding the first-generation units."[45]

Creating a Safety Culture

One of the more surprising post-Chernobyl findings was that Soviet reactors were marginally less safe than western reactors in their equipment, but much more dramatically lacking in what is known as "safety culture." This refers to the overall approach and routine beliefs of the entire industry toward safety issues, from facility designers to workers to regulators. In a well-established safety culture, all of the people involved in a nuclear technology should be committed to safety as a higher priority than efficiency, profits, or any other goal. "The 1979 accident at Three Mile Island and the 1986 accident at Chernobyl quickly dispelled the notion that nuclear power safety can be established through design and procedures and then forgotten," says engineer and nuclear safety culture specialist Charles R. Jones. "In view of the 1999 accident at Tokaimura, it is even more evident that a continuing nuclear safety

▼ A Nuclear Regulatory Commission inspector checks control room meters shortly after the 1979 Three Mile Island accident.

culture is required at each nuclear facility, whether it is a reactor plant, a fissile fuels plant, or a nuclear weapons facility."[46]

Among the traits Jones identifies as important to nuclear safety culture are adhering to procedures, ensuring that all the paperwork is filled out and signed, keeping lines of communication open between workers, managers, and executives, and notifying regulatory personnel when something goes wrong. In plants with a strong safety culture, managers train and supervise all plant workers, taking responsibility for work accomplished and not accomplished. Management should lead by example, showing a questioning attitude and a prudent approach.

Safety culture has become a prominent field of study in the nuclear industry. The IAEA has organized international conferences on the topic and national regulatory agencies have formed committees, run regular workshops, and conducted industry surveys on the topic. Dozens of research papers, and even some books, have been written on the topic. The NRC admits, however, that the concept remains amorphous and difficult to incorporate into direct regulations. As NRC Chairman Richard A. Meserve said at a November 2002 conference on nuclear safety:

The NRC does not purport to regulate safety culture directly. There is no NRC regulation that articulates an unambiguous direction to licensees to maintain an appropriate safety culture, although certainly aspects of safety culture are regulated. Moreover, the Commission does not have any performance indicators or other inspection tools that are routinely applied at plants to assess safety culture per se. Rather, the NRC seeks to ensure the existence of an appropriate safety culture through a variety of indirect means.[47]

The difficulty in regulating safety culture, and the need to rely on cor-

NUCLEAR EVENTS ONLINE

Learning about the latest nuclear incidents and accidents is now a matter of a few keystrokes. The online Nuclear Events Web-based System (NEWS) provides up-to-date information on the safety significance of events reported at nuclear installations worldwide. It covers accidents at nuclear power plants, research reactors, irradiation plants, and medical centers, as well as incidents that occur during the transport of radioactive material. For each event the system provides date, facility type, country, and a significance rating based on the accepted gauge of one for an anomaly to seven for a catastrophic accident. Clicking on the event title yields a short description of the accident. The online reporting system was restricted to authorized users from regulatory authorities and nuclear facilities until it was opened to the media and public in early 2003. It can be accessed at the IAEA's website (www-news.iaea.org).

porate attention to the topic, may be why serious accidents, like that at Tokaimura, are still being attributed primarily to the lack of a safety culture. Government officials and plant operators in Japan, charged Greenpeace spokesperson Shaun Burnie, "have a vested commercial interest in ignoring expensive safety standards." He went on to say that the "accident at Tokaimura confirms our fears: the entire safety culture within Japan is in crisis and the use of dangerous plutonium in reactors here will only increase the probability of a nuclear catastrophe."[48]

Nuclear Safety Goes Passive

Another new focus on nuclear safety relates to plant design and function. As a recent nuclear safety committee report has noted, "For future reactors, severe accidents will be addressed in the design stage."[49] Engineers have long recognized the advantage of having, for example, more standardized features to make licensing go more smoothly, and more resilient parts, so that these expensive facilities last longer than a mere thirty or forty years. Given the widespread public mistrust, especially in the United States, engineers have also been rethinking safety approaches.

The latest safety features, like those incorporated in the mid-1990s on two new nuclear plants opened in Japan, and a number of others under construction, are passive. This means operators do not need to make quick and complex decisions if something goes badly wrong. The system is set up so that nature takes over: A force, such as gravity or compressed gas, automatically closes a valve or performs a similar function that has the effect of stopping the emergency and avoiding an accident.

Passive safety systems are said to be inherently less risky than active systems by reducing the opportunity not only for human error but also for problems from the mechanical or electrical failure of pumps, fans, air conditioners, and the like. According to nuclear power plant builder Westinghouse Electric Company, one of its new-generation reactors, the AP1000, "has 50 percent fewer valves, 83 percent less piping, 87 percent less control cable, 35 percent fewer pumps and 50 percent less seismic building volume than a similarly sized conventional plant."[50] Such reductions not only promote safety but can also save time and money on equipment and construction.

▶ Lax safety procedures were a major factor at Tokaimura, where officials had to wait almost three weeks after the accident to measure possible remaining radiation.

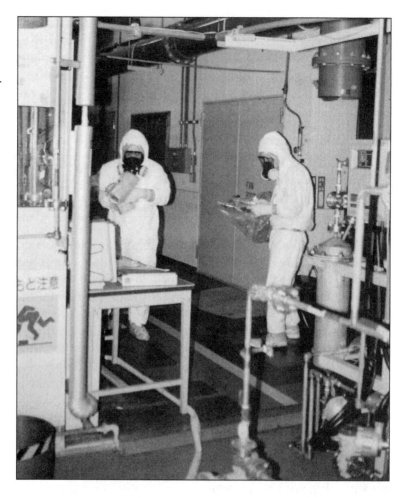

The concept is promising, especially given the "normal accident" theory of expected failures when systems become so complex. But how are the first passive safety reactors faring in the real world? The evidence suggests better, if not a total cure-all. The two new Japanese reactors, Kashiwazaki Kariwa-6 and -7, which power the world's largest nuclear plant, have not had any serious accidents since beginning operation in 1996. Critics of nuclear power note, however, that passive systems still need to be complemented by active systems, and that some factors remain out of human control. Many anti-nuclear activists believe, for example, that the Chashma nuclear reactor opened by Pakistan in 2000 is an accident waiting to happen. It was built in a highly active earthquake zone, on the potentially unstable banks of the Indus River, using relatively untested Chinese design and components.

Dealing with the Growing A-Bomb Club

Preventing the spread of nuclear bomb technology has been a major international concern in recent years. Since at least 1964, government officials have known that keeping the lid on atomic weapons would be difficult. That was when the U.S. government did the famous "Nth country experiment." Officials chose two young postdoctoral physics students, neither of which had any knowledge of nuclear technology. The officials challenged the nuclear novices to design a workable nuclear bomb without using any classified sources of information. It took three students (one in the original pair dropped out halfway through and was replaced) less than thirty months to succeed.

With the addition of Pakistan in 1998, the number of countries known to have tested nuclear weapons is now seven. North Korea claims to have built a few nuclear bombs. Israel is widely suspected to be an unannounced member of the club, having built perhaps as many as two hundred

▼ In September 2002, journalists tour Iraq's Tammuz nuclear reactor, which was bombed in 1981 and again in 1991.

nuclear warheads. In mid-2003 Iran, which has five research reactors and four unfinished power reactors, is thought to be on the verge of joining the atomic club.

Efforts to prevent the spread of nuclear weapons have taken two forms. One is military attack, which so far has been directed mainly at Iraq. Its attempts to build a nuclear plant that could generate weapons-grade plutonium were first quashed by Israeli bombing of an Iraqi nuclear construction site in 1981. The 2003 invasion of Iraq by U.S.-led forces has effectively ended any Iraqi nuclear threat for the foreseeable future. In the aftermath of the second Gulf War some U.S. government officials have said that a similar military attack on North Korea's nuclear facilities is a possibility.

The other approach has been diplomatic, mainly through the nuclear Non-Proliferation Treaty that was negotiated in the late 1960s. The treaty's membership has grown from forty-three original parties in 1970 to 187 today—virtually all of the countries of the world with the exception of Cuba, India, Israel, Pakistan, and North Korea (which withdrew in April 2003, the first such country to do so). Many of the signers, from South American powers like Brazil and Argentina, to Asian countries like Japan, have long had the expertise and enough plutonium from reactors to easily build an arsenal of nuclear bombs. Despite the continuing concerns regarding those countries that are not members, the treaty has arguably been a major factor in helping to prevent the spread of nuclear weapons and thus both their intentional and accidental use.

From Yucca Mountain to the Moon

Nuclear technology presents difficult long-term waste-related issues. "Fifty-nine years after the dawning of the nuclear age, not one country has managed to find anything more than a temporary resting place for its tons of nuclear detritus,"[51] a recent special report on nuclear power concluded. A number of countries are now decommissioning nuclear power plants, weapons factories, and submarines. Disposing of tons of contaminated concrete, steel, soil, and even whole structures is an engineering challenge of the first order. Nuclear waste can range from mildly toxic to extremely hazardous. The most highly radioactive materials need to be stashed safely away for tens of thousands, sometimes even *millions*, of years. The best nuclear-containing technology currently in use lasts a few decades.

Waste-related incidents are an often-overlooked category of nuclear accident. The 1967 accident of wind-borne radiation being dispersed from Lake Karachai, as well as the ongoing threat of the radioactive plume approaching a nearby river, can be attributed to the mishandling of nuclear wastes. Similar if not quite so horrendous episodes have happened in virtually every nuclear country of the world, and are likely to continue until engineers develop a truly successful method for dealing with nuclear waste.

Forgotten nuclear wastes can be extremely hazardous to workers or the public. In June 2001 nine workers in western Romania were dismantling a furnace in a smelting plant that had been closed and abandoned for more than a decade. Unaware of a source of cobalt-60, they were exposed to what Romanian authorities later admitted were huge doses of radiation, requiring the men to be hospitalized. The furnace area has since been sealed off. In an August 2002 incident, workers in a scrap yard in Rotterdam, the Netherlands, found nine stainless steel containers full of highly radioactive strontium-90. The material had been sent among scrap metal from Armenia.

For nuclear materials that have been more controlled, such as at nuclear power plants and weapons factories, the answer has been to encase wastes in casks and drums and bury or store them onsite. Container technology has improved in recent years but old containers have proven

▼ A container of radioactive plutonium waste, after being rejected by a Japanese nuclear plant and shipped back to England, is taken by train to England's Sellafield nuclear complex in September 2002.

DESIGNED TO REPEL

A 1991 government panel that researched the problems of keeping people away from nuclear waste sites for ten millennia included an astronomer, linguist (language specialist), archaeologist, environmental designer, and materials scientist. They developed a number of possible designs for the sites that were meant to convey "a sense of danger, foreboding, and dread without the use of language or pictures," and explicitly not suggesting "shelter, protection, or nurture." The designs included huge spikes that seemed to come from underneath the ground and a "landscape of thorns." Irregular, nongeometrical forms are also considered to show that humans do not value the place or embody it with their ideals.

▲ The spike field: Can its dangerous-looking shapes say "keep out" for ten millennia?

notoriously leaky. The United States has recently taken steps to begin construction of an underground storage facility at Yucca Mountain, Nevada. It would be a final resting home for spent nuclear fuel and high-level radioactive wastes currently stored at 131 sites around the nation. Even this solution, however, is not risk free, since it has the potential for accidents in transit and at the final site. For example, an Environmental Working Group study found that a serious rail accident involving nuclear waste headed for Yucca Mountain could expose hundreds of thousands of people in a major city to dangerous levels of radiation.

Even if Yucca Mountain opens, high-level nuclear waste will still have to be stored at facilities such as nuclear power plants for at least five years after removal from the reactor core so that it can become cool enough to ship. Moreover, alternative approaches to dealing with wastes—one proposal was loading it onto rockets and shooting it into the moon—present similar or even greater possibilities for future disasters.

How to Say "Keep Out" for 10,000 Years

Nuclear waste sites like the recently approved Yucca Mountain remain potentially deadly for thousands of years, creating an interesting practical dilemma: What is the best way to warn future generations—or even extraterrestrials—about the danger? The U.S. Department of Energy is consulting with various experts for advice. One potential warning reads: "Danger. Poisonous radioactive waste buried here. Do not dig or drill here before A.D. 12,000." Another proposed text is:

> This place is not a place of honor. No highly esteemed deed is commemorated here. Nothing valued is here. This place is a message and part of a system of messages. Pay attention to it! Sending this message was important to us. We considered ourselves to be a powerful culture.[52]

"Stay away" site designs and markers have also been proposed. "The very exercise of designing, building, and viewing the markers creates a powerful testimony addressed to today's society about the full environmental, social, and economic costs of using nuclear materials," noted the member of a panel formed to design nuclear waste sites. "We can never know if we indeed have successfully communicated with our descendants 400 generations removed, but we can, in any case, perhaps convey an important message to ourselves."[53]

Minimizing Nuclear Accidents

A greater emphasis on safety and preventing accidents has shown some promising results in recent years. The American nuclear power industry, for example, has improved significantly since 1990, when more than fifty events were classified as "significant" and plants averaged one "safety system actuation" per year. By 2000, according to the NRC, the average number of safety incidents per year decreased to about one for every three units.

Some other types of nuclear accidents may have also declined. At least among the two superpowers, the United States and Russia, lost nuclear bombs and fallout accidents clearly peaked during the Cold War. The fact that the contamination episodes at Goiania and Juarez during the mid-1980s have not been repeated may be an indication of increased corporate and government awareness for the need to maintain control over radioactive materials in medical and industrial devices.

Serious nuclear accidents of various types, however, remain a clear and present danger. The NRC recently admitted that for much of the past two decades it has been lax in dealing with safety culture problems at Millstone and a number of other New England nuclear power plants. With growing nuclear bomb proliferation in politically unstable areas, the risk increases of accidental nuclear explosions and lost nuclear material ending up in a dirty bomb used by terrorists. "Indeed accidental nuclear war remains a serious risk,"[54] contends a review article on nuclear weapons. The lack of a viable solution to the problem of containing and controlling nuclear waste suggests that waste-related accidents will continue, and possibly grow.

The long-lived nature of nuclear pollution, the inherent hazards of nuclear technology, and the potential for local disasters to become worldwide catastrophes may ultimately determine how willing the public is to accept growth in the existing nuclear industry, as well as to embrace new nuclear uses and their attendant risks.

Notes

Introduction: Disaster at Chernobyl

1. Quoted in David B. Kaplan, "When Incidents Are Accidents: The Silent Saga of the Nuclear Navy," *Oceans Magazine*, August 1983. http://oc.itgo.com.

2. *FEMA.gov*, Hazards, "Fact Sheet: Radiological Accidents." www.fema.gov.

Chapter 1: Accidents Waiting to Happen

3. Quoted in Robert del Tredici, *At Work in the Fields of the Bomb*. New York: Harper and Row, 1987, p. 134.

4. Quoted in Arnold S. Dion, "Acute Radiation Sickness," *Harry K. Daghlian, Jr.: America's First Peacetime Atom Bomb Fatality*. http://members.tripod.com.

5. Charles Perrow, *Complex Organizations: A Critical Essay*. New York: Random House, 1986, p. 146.

6. Quoted in "Chronology and Press Reports of the Tokaimura Criticality," *Institute for Science and International Security*. www.isis-online.org.

7. "Chronology," *Institute for Science and International Security*.

8. *U.S. Nuclear Regulatory Commission*, Who We Are, Our History, "A Short History of Nuclear Regulation, 1946–1999." www.nrc.gov.

Chapter 2: From Meltdowns to Leaks

9. Charles Perrow, *Normal Accidents: Living with High-Risk Technologies*. Princeton, NJ: Princeton University Press, 1999, p. 16.

10. Quoted in John G. Fuller, *We Almost Lost Detroit*. New York: Reader's Digest, 1975, p. 86.

11. Kenneth D. Bergeron, *Tritium on Ice: The Dangerous New Alliance of Nuclear Weapons and Nuclear Power*. Cambridge, MA: MIT Press, 2002, p. 144.

12. Bergeron, *Tritium on Ice*, p. 144.

13. Bergeron, *Tritium on Ice*, p. 51.

14. Perrow, *Normal Accidents*, p. 16.

15. Quoted in Mike Edwards, "Chernobyl—One Year After," *National Geographic,* May 1987, p. 644.

16. *Union of Concerned Scientists*, Clean Energy, "Nuclear Plant Risk Studies: Failing the Grade." www.ucsusa.org.

17. Perrow, *Normal Accidents*, p. 33.

Chapter 3: Weapons of Mass Destruction

18. Peter Goin, *Nuclear Landscapes.* Baltimore, MD: John Hopkins University Press, 1991, p. 14.

19. *Trinity Atomic Web Site,* "The Soviet Nuclear Weapons Program." http://nuketesting.enviroweb.org.

20. del Tredici, *At Work in the Fields of the Bomb*, p. 35.

21. Cat Lazaroff, "Nuclear Testing Caused Cancers Around the Globe," *Green Cross International.* www.greencrossinternational.net.

22. Quoted in Allan Thompson, "Living at Ground Zero," *Canadian Centres for Teaching Peace.* www.peace.ca.

23. Thompson, "Living at Ground Zero," *Canadian Centres for Teaching Peace.*

24. Jack Niedenthal, "Paradise Lost—'For the Good of Mankind,'" *Guardian Unlimited.* www.guardian.co.uk.

25. Katherine N. Probst, Carolyn A. Pilling, and Karen T. Dunn, "Cleaning Up the Nuclear Weapons Complex: Exploring New Approaches." Washington, DC: Resources for the Future, 1996, p. 22.

26. Quoted in David Burnham, "CIA Papers Released to Nader Tell of 2 Soviet Nuclear Accidents," *New York Times*, November 26, 1977. www.mindfully.org.

27. David Hoffman, "Wastes of War: Radioactivity Threatens a Mighty River," *Washington Post*, August 17, 1998. www.washingtonpost.com.

28. Kaplan, "When Incidents Are Accidents," *Oceans Magazine.*

29. *The Brookings Institution*, "Atomic Audit: The Costs and Consequences of U.S. Nuclear Weapons Since 1940." www.brook.edu.

Chapter 4: Risky Business

30. Douglas Holdstock and Lis Waterston, "Nuclear Weapons, a Continuing Threat," *Lancet*, April 29, 2000, p. 1545.

31. Chris Shuey, "Contaminant Loading on the Puerco River: A Historical Overview," *Southwest Research and Information Center*. www.sric.org.

32. Robert C. Ricks et al., "REAC/TS Radiation Accident Registry: Update of Accidents in the United States." Oak Ridge, TN: Radiation Emergency Assistance Center/Training Site, 2000, p. 2.

33. Istvan Turai and Katalin Veress, "Radiation Accidents: Occurrence, Types, Consequences, Medical Management, and the Lessons to Be Learned," *Central European Journal of Occupational and Environmental Medicine*, vol. 7, no. 1, pp. 3–14.

34. Alex Neifert, "Case Study: Accidental Leakage of Cesium-137 in Goiania, Brazil, in 1987," *Medical NBC Online*. www.nbc-med.org.

35. Quoted in Neifert, "Case Study," *Medical NBC Online*.

36. Neifert, "Case Study," *Medical NBC Online*.

37. Thomas Nilsen, "Nuclear Lighthouses to Be Replaced," *Bellona*. www.bellona.no.

38. *Mapscience.org*, "EWG Nuclear Waste Route Atlas." www.mapscience.org.

Chapter 5: Nuclear 911: Rescue and Response

39. Quoted in Pavel Polityuk, "Update: Ukraine, Neighbours Commemorate Chernobyl Victims," *Planet Ark*, April 27, 2000. www.planetark.org.

40. Quoted in Andrey Illesh, *Chernobyl: A Russian Journalist's Eyewitness Account*. New York: Richardson & Steirman, 1987, p. 124.

41. Jim Green, "Research Reactor Accidents," *The Sustainable Energy and Anti-Uranium Service*. www.sea-us.org.au.

42. Quoted in "Project Tasks 3 & 4 Final Draft Report," *Reconstruction of Historical Rocky Flats Operations & Identification of Release Points*. ChemRisk/Colorado Department of Health, 1992, p. 229.

43. Quoted in "Project Tasks," *Reconstruction of Historical Rocky Flats Operations & Identification of Release Points*, p. 235.

44. Quoted in Andrei Ivanov and Judith Perera, "Radioactive Lake Threatens Arctic Disaster," *OneWorld.net*. www.oneworld.net.

Chapter 6: The Challenge of Preventing Nuclear Accidents

45. Luis Lederman, "Safety of RBMK Reactors: Setting the Technical Framework," *International Atomic Energy Agency*. www.iaea.org.

46. Charles R. Jones, "Introduction to Nuclear Safety Culture," *Technidigm*. www.technidigm.org.

47. Richard A. Meserve, "Safety Culture: An NRC Perspective," *U.S. Nuclear Regulatory Commission*. www.nrc.gov.

48. Quoted in *Greenpeace.org*, "Tokaimura Nuclear Accident Exposes Japan's Failed Safety Culture on Eve of Arrival of Plutonium Shipment." www.greenpeace.org.

49. *Nuclear Energy Agency*, "OECD Countries Reaffirm Their Consensus on the Prevention of Severe Nuclear Accidents." www.nea.fr.

50. *Westinghouse*, "AP1000." www.ap1000.westinghouse.com.

51. Glenn Zorpette, "Canned Heat," *IEEE Spectrum Online*. www.spectrum.ieee.org.

52. "Expert Judgement on Markers to Deter Inadvertent Human Intrusion into the Waste Isolation Pilot Plant," Sandia National Laboratories, SAND92-1382, 1992.

53. Quoted in "Expert Judgement on Markers," Sandia National Laboratories.

54. Holdstock and Waterston, "Nuclear Weapons," *Lancet*, p. 1544.

Glossary

atomic bomb: An explosive device whose power is generated by the release of atomic energy from the splitting of nuclei of elements such as uranium or plutonium; a fission bomb.

background radiation: Naturally occurring radiation such as humans are exposed to from cosmic rays originating in outer space and from radioactive elements in soil and water.

containment building: A building with very thick walls that surrounds a nuclear reactor and serves as a protection against accidental release of radiation into the environment.

control rods: Pipes filled with a substance such as carbon that can be placed near the fuel rods in a nuclear reactor to help neutralize a nuclear reaction and thus slow it down or stop it.

cooling towers: The huge, hourglass-shaped structures that disperse heat from a nuclear reactor by releasing evaporated water into the air.

core: The central part of a nuclear reactor and the site of the nuclear fuel that ultimately produces heat.

curie: A unit of radioactivity, named after the Polish-born French chemist Marie Curie, equal to the radiation emitted by one gram of radium per second.

dirty bomb: A conventional (nonnuclear) explosive that contains radioactive material and thus spreads radioactive contamination when triggered.

dosimeter: A device, typically clipped to clothing, which records the body's level of radiation exposure.

fallout: Radioactive particles, as from a nuclear accident or bomb test, that drop from the atmosphere to the ground.

fission: The splitting of the nuclei of atoms capable of releasing huge quantities of nuclear energy.

fuel rods: Slender, hollow pipes typically filled with pellets of uranium fuel that power a nuclear reactor; fuel rods are bundled into "fuel assemblies" before being loaded into the reactor core.

fusion: The union of the nuclei of atoms capable of releasing huge quantities of nuclear energy.

hydrogen bomb: An explosive device whose power is generated by the release of atomic energy from the fusing of nuclei of elements such as hydrogen; a fusion bomb.

ionizing radiation: Energy in the form of particles, such as alpha and beta particles, or waves, such as gamma waves and X rays, that the nucleus of an unstable atom emits due to radioactive decay.

meltdown: A runaway accidental reaction within a nuclear reactor that results in overheating of the nuclear fuel and the melting of the core.

nuclear bomb: An atomic (fission), hydrogen (fusion), or combination fission/fusion weapon.

nuclear reactor: A device that uses nuclear fuel and some controlling materials to sustain a nuclear reaction.

plutonium: A mostly human-made element produced from uranium in a nuclear reactor and used to make nuclear weapons.

rad: Short for "radiation absorbed dose," a unit to measure how much ionizing radiation has been absorbed by a certain amount of body tissue, for example.

rem: Short for "rad equivalent man," a dose unit found by multiplying rads by certain modifying factors.

spent nuclear fuel: Uranium or other fuel that has been used in a reactor for some time and thus has lost most of its useful energy; it nevertheless remains highly radioactive.

uranium: A heavy, metallic, radioactive element that is used to fuel most nuclear reactors.

For Further Reading

Books

John G. Fuller, *We Almost Lost Detroit.* New York: Reader's Digest, 1975. A lively recounting of a number of early nuclear accidents.

Wilborn Hampton, *Meltdown: A Race Against Nuclear Disaster at Three Mile Island.* Cambridge, MA: Candlewick Press, 2001. A reporter's-eye view of the 1979 accident.

Don Nardo, *Chernobyl.* San Diego: Lucent Books, 1990. A readable, illustrated entry in the World Disasters series.

Periodicals

Mike Edwards, "Chernobyl—One Year After," *National Geographic,* May 1987.

———, "Living With the Monster—Chornobyl," *National Geographic,* August 1994.

Douglas Holdstock and Lis Waterston, "Nuclear Weapons, a Continuing Threat," *Lancet,* April 29, 2000.

Ken Silverstein, "Tale of the Radioactive Boy Scout," *Harper's Magazine,* November 1998.

Internet Sources

David Hoffman, "Wastes of War: Radioactivity Threatens a Mighty River," *Washington Post,* August 17, 1998. www.washingtonpost.com.

Richard A. Meserve, "Safety Culture: An NRC Perspective," *U.S. Nuclear Regulatory Commission.* www.nrc.gov.

Jack Niedenthal, "Paradise Lost—'For the Good of Mankind,'" *Guardian Unlimited.* www.guardian.co.uk.

Thomas Nilsen, "Nuclear Lighthouses to Be Replaced," *Bellona.* www.bellna.no.

Trinity Atomic Web Site, "The Soviet Nuclear Weapons Program." http://nuketesting.enviroweb.org.

U.S. Nuclear Regulatory Commission, Who We Are, Our History, "A Short History of Nuclear Regulation, 1946–1999." www.nrc.gov.

Washington Post, "Three Mile Island: Special Report," March 28, 1989. www.washingtonpost.com.

Websites

Centers for Disease Control (www.cdc.gov). Offers useful background information on the health effects of radiation.

International Atomic Energy Agency (www.iaea.org). Provides up-to-date news relating to regulations and programs as well as features such as an online nuclear event reporting system.

Nuclearfiles.org (www.nuclearfiles.org). This website of the Nuclear Age Peace Foundation features news, time lines, resources, study guides, and more.

U.S. Nuclear Regulatory Commission (www.nrc.gov). A compendium of background information as well as documents, news, and fact sheets.

Works Consulted

Books

Kenneth D. Bergeron, *Tritium on Ice: The Dangerous New Alliance of Nuclear Weapons and Nuclear Power.* Cambridge, MA: MIT Press, 2002. A penetrating look at the potential consequences of merging civilian and military uses of nuclear technology.

Mike Davis, *Dead Cities.* New York: The New Press, 2002. Contains a hard-hitting chapter on nuclear devastation of the American west.

Peter Goin, *Nuclear Landscapes.* Baltimore, MD: Johns Hopkins University Press, 1991. Striking images of nuclear test sites, weapons complexes, and waste facilities.

Andrey Illesh, *Chernobyl: A Russian Journalist's Eyewitness Account.* New York: Richardson & Steirman, 1987. A dramatic account of history's worst nuclear accident.

Charles Perrow, *Complex Organizations: A Critical Essay.* New York: Random House, 1986. Offers provocative insights into how things can go wrong even in the best-run industries.

———, *Normal Accidents: Living with High-Risk Technologies.* Princeton, NJ: Princeton University Press, 1999. Reveals why nuclear catastrophes are likely.

D.J. Peterson, *Troubled Lands: The Legacy of Soviet Environmental Destruction.* Boulder, CO: Rand, 1993. A comprehensive recounting of nuclear devastation in Russia.

Robert del Tredici, *At Work in the Fields of the Bomb.* New York: Harper and Row, 1987. Photographs and text document major events in nuclear history, from Hiroshima to Chernobyl.

Periodicals

Charles E. Cobb Jr., "Living with Radiation," *National Geographic*, April 1989.

"The Human Consequences of the Chernobyl Nuclear Accident: A Strategy for Recovery." New York: United Nations, January 25, 2002.

Michael E. Long, "Half Life: The Lethal Legacy of America's Nuclear Waste," *National Geographic*, July 2002.

Najmedin Meshkati, "Human Factors in Large-Scale Technological Systems' Accidents: Three Mile Island, Bhopal, Chernobyl," *Industrial Crisis Quarterly*, vol. 5, 1991.

Katherine N. Probst, Carolyn A. Pilling, and Karen T. Dunn, "Cleaning Up the Nuclear Weapons Complex: Exploring New Approaches." Washington, DC: Resources for the Future, 1996.

"Project Tasks 3 & 4 Final Draft Report," *Reconstruction of Historical Rocky Flats Operations & Identification of Release Points*. ChemRisk/Colorado Department of Health, 1992.

Robert C. Ricks et al., "REAC/TS Radiation Accident Registry: Update of Accidents in the United States." Oak Ridge, TN: Radiation Emergency Assistance Center/Training Site, 2000.

Sandia National Laboratories, "Expert Judgement on Markers to Deter Inadvertent Human Intrusion into the Waste Isolation Pilot Plant," SAND92-1382, 1992.

Istvan Turai and Katalin Veress, "Radiation Accidents: Occurrence, Types, Consequences, Medical Management, and the Lessons to Be Learned," *Central European Journal of Occupational and Environmental Medicine*, vol. 7, no. 1.

Kenneth F. Weaver, "The Promise and Peril of Nuclear Energy," *National Geographic*, April 1979.

Richard Wiles and James R. Cox, "What If . . . Nuclear Waste Accident Scenarios in the United States." Washington, DC: Environmental Working Group, 2002.

Internet Sources

Robert Roy Britt, "Nuclear Power Poised for Re-Entry into Space," Technology, *Space.com*. www.space.com.

The Brookings Institution, "Atomic Audit: The Costs and Consequences of U.S. Nuclear Weapons Since 1940." www.brook.edu.

David Burnham, "CIA Papers Released to Nader Tell of 2 Soviet Nuclear Accidents," *New York Times*, November 26, 1977. www.mindfully.org.

Arnold S. Dion, "Acute Radiation Sickness," *Harry K. Daghlian, Jr.: America's First Peacetime Atom Bomb Fatality.* http://members.tripod.com.

FEMA.gov, Hazards, "Fact Sheet: Radiological Accidents." www.fema.gov.

Jim Green, "Research Reactor Accidents," *The Sustainable Energy and Anti-Uranium Service.* www.sea-us.org.au.

Greenpeace.org, "Tokaimura Nuclear Accident Exposes Japan's Failed Safety Culture on Eve of Arrival of Plutonium Shipment." www.greenpeace.org.

Institute for Science and International Security, "Chronology and Press Reports of the Tokaimura Criticality." www.isis-online.org.

Andrei Ivanov and Judith Perera, "Radioactive Lake Threatens Arctic Disaster," *OneWorld.net*. www.oneworld.net.

Charles R. Jones, "Introduction to Nuclear Safety Culture," *Technidigm*. www.technidigm.org.

David B. Kaplan, "When Incidents Are Accidents: The Silent Saga of the Nuclear Navy," *Oceans Magazine*, August 1983. http://ic.itgo.com.

Cat Lazaroff, "Nuclear Testing Caused Cancers Around the Globe," *Green Cross International*. www.greencrossinternational.net.

Luis Lederman, "Safety of RBMK Reactors: Setting the Technical Framework," *International Atomic Energy Agency*. www.iaea.org.

Mapscience.org, "EWG Nuclear Waste Route Atlas." www.mapscience.org.

NASA SpaceLink, "NASA Fact Sheet: Past Space Nuclear Power System Accidents." http://spacelink.nasa.gov.

Alex Neifert, "Case Study: Accidental Leakage of Cesium-137 in Goiania, Brazil, in 1987," *Medical NBC Online*. www.nbc-med.org.

Nuclear Energy Agency, "OECD Countries Reaffirm Their Consensus on the Prevention of Severe Nuclear Accidents." www.nea.fr.

Pavel Polityuk, "Update: Ukraine, Neighbours Commemorate Chernobyl Victims," *Planet Ark*, April 27, 2000. www.planetark.org.

Chris Shuey, "Contaminant Loading on the Puerco River: A Historical Overview," *Southwest Research and Information Center*. www.sric.org.

Allan Thompson, "Living at Ground Zero," *Canadian Centres for Teaching Peace*. www.peace.ca.

Union of Concerned Scientists, Clean Energy, "Nuclear Plant Risk Studies: Failing the Grade." www.ucsusa.org.

Westinghouse, "AP1000." www.ap1000.westinghouse.com.

Glenn Zorpette, "Canned Heat," *IEEE Spectrum Online*. www.spectrum.ieee.org.

Websites

Bellona Foundation (www.bellona.no). This Oslo, Norway-based environmental group has excellent sections on the nuclear threat.

Bulletin of the Atomic Scientists (www.thebulletin.org). Thorough news and background with numerous feature articles.

Center for Defense Information (www.cdi.org). Offers reliable facts and figures, news, and analysis on nuclear weapons and testing.

Trinity Atomic Web Site (http://nuketesting.enviroweb.org). Provides a range of historic documents, photos, and information relating to nuclear weapons history, technology, and consequences (including accidents).

Index

Picture Credits

About the Author

Mark Mayell is a freelance writer and editor who has authored nonfiction books on health and travel, as well as numerous magazine articles. He lives with his wife and two children in Wellesley, Massachusetts.